D0904679

The Canadian Centre for Energy Information

All about energy. All in one place.

As concerns about the environment and economy increase, so too does the need for balanced and credible information about energy in Canada. The Canadian Centre for Energy Information was created in 2002 to meet that need.

We believe an informed and educated public better understands and supports energy policy and regulatory choices, makes better business decisions related to energy, chooses careers in energy, invests in energy and uses energy wisely.

Supported by research and vetted by reputable, independent sources, we are Canada's key resource for credible, up-to-date energy information. Our web portal at www.centreforenergy.com covers the Canadian energy system from the mainstays of oil, natural gas, coal, nuclear and hydropower through to solar, wind, thermal, biomass, geothermal and fuel cells.

On January 1, 2003, the Petroleum Communications Foundation became part of the Centre for Energy. We would like to acknowledge the contribution made by that organization in the development of *Our Petroleum Challenge.*

About this book

This book provides a general introduction to Canada's crude oil and natural gas industry.

Section 1 presents an overview of the nation's crude oil and natural gas resources and the role they play in modern society.

Section 2 describes in more detail the steps involved in finding, producing, processing, transporting, refining, selling and using petroleum products.

Section 3 discusses the challenges and opportunities facing the industry in the 21st century.

A bibliography provides sources for further information, and an index helps readers to locate topics in the text. There is also a metric conversion table. The glossary at the back defines specialized industry terms.

About the cover

The people who make it all happen, access to resources, technological development, environmental stewardship...the cover of *Our Petroleum Challenge* symbolically represents key players and issues involved in facing the challenge of sustaining our energy resources into the 21st century.

Photos on the front and back covers provided courtesy of Brian Harder.

Key definitions

Hydrocarbons are compounds of hydrogen and carbon. The simplest hydrocarbon is methane (CH_4), composed of one carbon atom and four hydrogen atoms.

Natural gas is mainly methane, although it can occur in nature as a mixture with other hydrocarbons such as ethane, propane, butane and pentane and with other substances such as carbon dioxide, nitrogen, sulphur compounds and/or helium. These components are separated from the methane at processing plants located near the producing fields.

Crude oil is a naturally occurring liquid mixture of hydrocarbons. It typically includes complex hydrocarbon molecules – long chains and rings of hydrogen and carbon atoms. The liquid hydrocarbons may be mixed with natural gas, carbon dioxide, saltwater, sulphur compounds and sand. Most of these substances are separated from the liquid hydrocarbons at field processing facilities called batteries.

Bitumen is a semi-solid hydrocarbon mixture. The bitumen in Alberta's oil sands is the world's largest known hydrocarbon resource.

Gasoline is a complex mixture of relatively volatile hydrocarbons, with or without small quantities of additives, suitable for use in spark-ignition engines.

Petroleum is a general term for all the naturally occurring hydrocarbons – natural gas, natural gas liquids, crude oil and bitumen.

Natural gas liquids are ethane, propane, butane and condensates (pentanes and heavier hydrocarbons) that are often found along with natural gas; some of these hydrocarbons are liquid only at low temperatures or under pressure.

Liquefied natural gas (LNG) is supercooled natural gas that is maintained as a liquid at -160°C. LNG occupies 1/640th of its original volume and is therefore easier to transport if pipelines cannot be used.

Fluids are either liquids or gases – substances whose molecules move freely past one another and that have the tendency to assume the shape of a container. Most forms of petroleum, except some bitumen, are fluids.

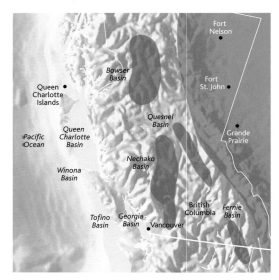

OFFSHORE WESTERN CANADA

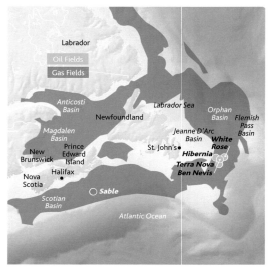

OFFSHORE EASTERN CANADA

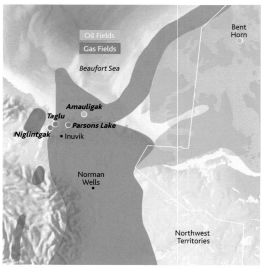

ARCTIC REGION

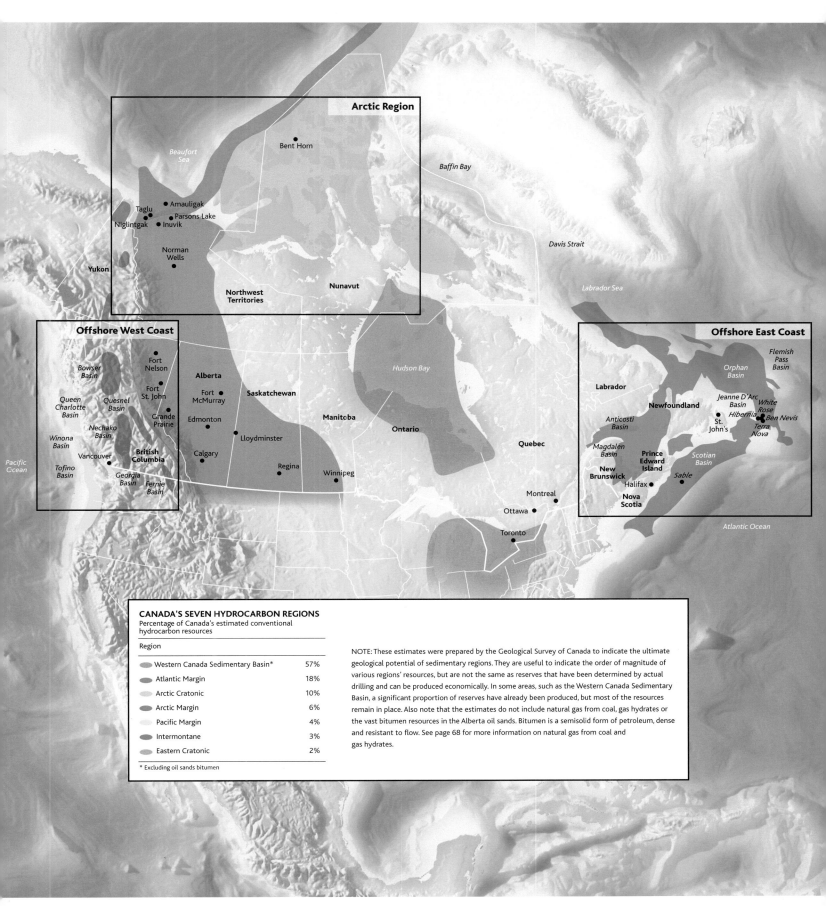

Arctic Region

Beaufort *Sea*

Bent Horn

Baffin Bay

Taglu
Amauligak
Parsons Lake
Niglintgak
Inuvik

Davis Strait

Norman
Wells

Yukon

Northwest
Territories
Nunavut

Labrador Sea

Offshore West Coast

Offshore East Coast

Bowser
Basin

Fort
Nelson

Flemish
Pass
Basin

Orphan
Basin

Queen
Charlotte
Basin

Quesnel
Basin

Fort
St. John

Alberta

Labrador

Jeanne D'Arc
Basin
White
Rose

Nechako
Basin

Grande
Prairie

Fort
McMurray

Saskatchewan

Newfoundland

Anticosti
Basin

Hibernia
Ben Nevis

Winona
Basin

Edmonton

St.
John's

Terra
Nova

Vancouver

**British
Columbia**

Lloydminster

Manitoba

Hudson Bay

Magdalen
Basin

*Pacific
Ocean*

Tofino
Basin

Calgary

Ontario

**New
Brunswick**

**Prince
Edward
Island**

Scotian
Basin

*Georgia
Basin*

*Fernie
Basin*

Regina

Winnipeg

Quebec

Halifax

Sable

**Nova
Scotia**

Montreal

Ottawa

Atlantic Ocean

Toronto

CANADA'S SEVEN HYDROCARBON REGIONS
Percentage of Canada's estimated conventional
hydrocarbon resources

Region

Western Canada Sedimentary Basin*		57%
Atlantic Margin		18%
Arctic Cratonic		10%
Arctic Margin		6%
Pacific Margin		4%
Intermontane		3%
Eastern Cratonic		2%

* Excluding oil sands bitumen

NOTE: These estimates were prepared by the Geological Survey of Canada to indicate the ultimate
geological potential of sedimentary regions. They are useful to indicate the order of magnitude of
various regions' resources, but are not the same as reserves that have been determined by actual
drilling and can be produced economically. In some areas, such as the Western Canada Sedimentary
Basin, a significant proportion of reserves have already been produced, but most of the resources
remain in place. Also note that the estimates do not include natural gas from coal, gas hydrates or
the vast bitumen resources in the Alberta oil sands. Bitumen is a semisolid form of petroleum, dense
and resistant to flow. See page 68 for more information on natural gas from coal and
gas hydrates.

Source: Geological Survey of Canada

Our Petroleum Challenge
Sustainability into the 21st Century
Seventh Edition

N.B. Sidebars are shown in italics.

Maps, tables and illustrations

Section 1
Our Hydrocarbon Legacy

Canadians rely on petroleum to provide gasoline and diesel fuel for cars, trucks, buses, trains and boats, jet fuel for airplanes, and natural gas to heat homes, businesses and public buildings. Countless other products around us are also made from crude oil and natural gas – such as plastics, synthetic rubber, lubricants, paints, solvents, asphalt paving and roofing, insulation and fertilizers.

The industry that makes all this possible is vast and complex – a long chain of enterprises and facilities connecting fluids hidden in the pores of buried rocks to the home furnace and the local retail outlet. People, knowledge and technology are the industry's key assets.

MAJOR SUPPLIERS OF CRUDE OIL AND REFINED PRODUCTS TO THE UNITED STATES (thousands of cubic metres per day)

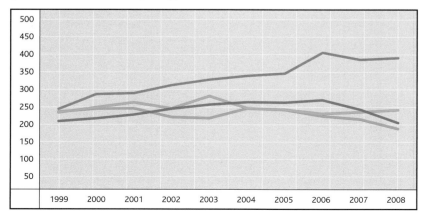

Source: Energy Information Administration

CANADA   MEXICO
SAUDI ARABIA   VENEZUELA

Modern industrial economies around the world depend on petroleum, and Canada is one of the few countries that produces more oil and natural gas than its people consume. International sales of crude oil and natural gas make a major contribution to the Canadian economy. By contrast, the United States imports more than half of its crude oil requirements and about one-sixth of its natural gas supply. From 2000 to the present, Canada was the largest single foreign supplier of crude oil and refined products to the United States, ahead of Saudi Arabia, Mexico and Venezuela, and Canada is by far the largest foreign supplier of natural gas to the United States.

Canada achieved its position in the world oil and gas industry due to events that occurred on two very different time scales. During a half-billion years of Earth's history, nature formed hydrocarbons in the types of sedimentary rocks that are under parts of every province and territory.

Photos courtesy of ConocoPhillips, Petro-Canada, Shell Canada, Syncrude Canada Ltd. and Tesco Corporation

Over the past century and a half, Canadians became skilled in finding, extracting, processing and transporting this buried wealth. Canadian companies and individuals have played a role in developing petroleum resources at home and around the world.

There are both costs and benefits to producing and using crude oil and natural gas. As each cubic metre is consumed, companies must search for new resources to replace the production. Equally important, there is the potential for adverse effects on land, water, air, plants and animals, and human health and safety. The benefits may be enjoyed in one region, while the costs are borne in another. Oil and gas development can also positively or negatively affect Aboriginal communities and others in rural and remote areas. Government regulation and public consultation are key tools in managing the social and environmental effects of petroleum development and making sure that economic benefits are achieved.

Section 1 provides an overview of the role that the oil and gas industry plays in the daily lives of Canadians and how it affects our economy, society and environment. First, however, it is important to understand the industry's geological and historical bases.

The challenge

Canada is fortunate to have a vast endowment of petroleum resources. Developing these resources provides hundreds of thousands of jobs for Canadians and contributes to our national wealth and trade balance.

Crude oil and natural gas, and the products derived from them, play a vital role in almost every aspect of our economy and lifestyle.

Our challenge is to develop petroleum resources responsibly and to use them wisely, considering the needs of future generations as well as our own.

Did you know?

About 25 per cent of Canadian natural gas is used for home heating.

Illustration courtesy of Dennis Budgen

Geologic time

The Earth is about 4 ½ billion years old. The earliest of the sediments that produced almost all crude oil and natural gas were deposited about 560 million years ago. To understand the time scale involved, imagine that one second equals one year. If you started counting one number per second, you would reach one million in 11 ½ days, and one billion in 31 ½ years. On this accelerated time scale, petroleum resources have been accumulating for more than 16 years and the Canadian petroleum industry, now more than 150 years old, has been around for 2 ½ minutes.

The Earth is not the fixed, solid mass we usually envision. It is actually a sphere of solids and molten rock fluids that are gradually but continuously moving and changing. For example, South America is drifting away from Africa at about the speed your fingernails grow. Earthquakes and volcanoes are reminders of the Earth's instability and changing face. The planet's crust is divided into numerous tectonic plates. These plates push against and override each other, rise and fall, tilt and slide, buckle and crumple, break apart and merge together. As a result, sediments from the bottom of ancient seas can today be found in rocks on the tops of mountains. In fact, the summit of Mount Everest at 8,850 metres is marine limestone, formed from coral reefs in an ancient sea.

Not written in stone

The description on these pages is based on the organic theory of the origins of petroleum – that the hydrocarbons originated from biological processes. The organic theory is the most widely accepted among Canadian geologists, and it appears to explain how most of the world's crude oil and natural gas reservoirs ended up in the places where they have been found. However, there are other theories, including the inorganic theory that maintains some hydrocarbons were trapped inside the Earth during the planet's formation and are slowly moving towards the surface. Scientists continue to explore the possibility that some hydrocarbons might be formed from non-fossil sources and might be found at greater depths than known crude oil and natural gas resources. Laboratory experiments and deep drilling have provided some evidence in support of this theory.

Origins of crude oil and natural gas

In photosynthesis, plants absorb solar energy and use it to convert carbon dioxide and water into oxygen and sugar. Additional processes convert sugar into starch and cellulose. These carbohydrates and other organic materials from decaying organisms eventually settle on land or on the bottoms of lakes and seas.

As the organic materials become more deeply buried, heat and pressure transform them into solid, liquid or gaseous hydrocarbons known as fossil fuels – coal, crude oil or natural gas. Coal is formed from the remains of terrestrial (land-based) plants. Peat moss is an example of the type of material that becomes coal. Crude oil is typically derived from marine (water-based) plants and animals, mainly algae, that have been gently "cooked" for at least one million years at a temperature between 50° and 150° C.

Natural gas can be formed from almost any marine or terrestrial organic materials, under a wide variety of temperatures and pressures. Even landfill sites produce methane through bacterial action on organic waste. Landfill gas is approximately 50 per cent methane and 50 per cent carbon dioxide with trace amounts of nitrogen, oxygen, sulphur compounds and volatile organic compounds.

Due to the force of gravity and the pressures created by the overlying rock layers, crude oil and natural gas seldom stay in the source rock in which they are formed. Instead, they migrate through the underground layers of sedimentary rocks until they either escape at the surface or are trapped by a barrier of less permeable rock.

Most of the world's petroleum has been found trapped in porous rocks under a layer of relatively impermeable rock.

Oil seep near Canada's first oil well in Ontario.

Photo by Robert Bott

In such reservoirs, the crude oil and natural gas do not pool in underground "lakes" but are held in the pores and fractures of rock–like water in a sponge. These reservoirs are often long distances away from the original source.

A seep occurs when hydrocarbons migrate to the Earth's surface. Over time, huge amounts of these hydrocarbons have been degraded by bacteria or escaped into the atmosphere. Flowing water can also wash away hydrocarbons. Sometimes only the lighter, more volatile compounds are removed, leaving behind reservoirs of heavier types of crude oil.

The Alberta oil sands are different from most petroleum reservoirs, in both size and how they were formed. About 50 million years ago, huge volumes of crude oil migrated northeastward and upward through more than 100 kilometres of rock until they reached large areas of porous sandstone at or near the surface. Bacteria then degraded the hydrocarbons for millions of years. Geologists believe the original volume of crude oil digested by the micro-organisms was at least two or three times larger than what now remains as bitumen, and yet the Alberta oil sands are still the world's largest known hydrocarbon resource.

Bacteria usually degrade the simplest hydrocarbons first, converting them into carbon dioxide and water, and leave behind the big hydrocarbon molecules like those in asphalt and other substances such as nickel that cannot be digested. The bacteria may also modify some of the simpler sulphur molecules, leaving complex sulphur compounds. As a result, there are more heavy hydrocarbons, complex sulphur compounds and metals in bitumen than in conventional crude oil. This makes extraction and processing more difficult and expensive.

Where are crude oil and natural gas found?

Crude oil and natural gas are found in sedimentary rocks formed over millions of years by the accumulation in sedimentary basins of sand, silt and the remains of plants and animals. Canada has seven distinct regions of sedimentary rocks. Every province and territory includes at least a portion of a sedimentary basin. (See maps of sedimentary regions in front of book.)

The most productive hydrocarbon area in Canada is the Western Canada Sedimentary Basin, which includes most of Alberta and Saskatchewan and parts of British Columbia, Manitoba, Yukon and the Northwest Territories. The majority of current crude oil and natural gas exploration and production activities are concentrated in this basin. In 2003, the Western Canada Sedimentary Basin accounted for about 87 per cent of Canada's crude oil and 97 per cent of natural gas production. The Geological Survey of Canada (GSC) estimates the basin contained 57 per cent of Canada's original conventional petroleum resources. This figure does not include the non-conventional bitumen of the Alberta oil sands, the world's largest known petroleum resource. The largest oil sands deposits are in northeastern Alberta near Fort McMurray, but there are also bitumen deposits in other northeastern and northwestern areas of the province.

The Atlantic Margin extends along the East Coast from offshore U.S. waters to the coast of Baffin Island. This area is the site of major offshore crude oil and natural gas deposits discovered since the 1970s. The region's first crude oil production occurred between 1992 and 1999 from the Panuke and Cohasset oilfields off Nova Scotia, followed by much larger oil production starting in 1997 from the Hibernia project off Newfoundland and Labrador. Terra Nova and White Rose, two more offshore projects, began oil production in 2002 and 2005. The region's first natural gas production began in 1999 from the Sable Offshore Energy Project off Nova Scotia. The GSC estimates that the Atlantic Margin contained 18 per cent of Canada's original conventional petroleum resources. This region is an increasingly important contributor to the nation's petroleum supply.

WESTERN CANADA SEDIMENTARY BASIN

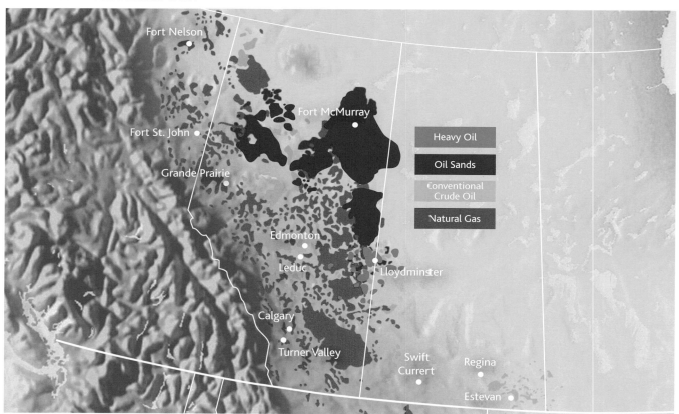

In 2007, the Western Canada Sedimentary Basin accounted for about 88.5 per cent of Canada's crude oil production and 97.4 per cent of Canada's natural gas production.

©Canadian Centre for Energy Information 2009

Substantial crude oil and natural gas resources have also been identified in the Arctic Islands, Beaufort Sea and Mackenzie Valley, but development has been slow due to Aboriginal land claims, the long distance from markets and the absence of pipeline systems. Two regions of sedimentary rocks – the Arctic Margin and the Arctic Cratonic basins – are estimated to hold 16 per cent of Canada's conventional petroleum resources. (Cratonic rocks are those that have been relatively undisturbed since pre-Cambrian times, generally found in interior areas of the continent.) The only crude oil production to date has consisted of tanker shipments between 1985 and 1996 from the Bent Horn well in the Arctic Islands. Since 1999, natural gas has also been produced in the Mackenzie Delta to supply the community of Inuvik 50 kilometres away.

Eastern Cratonic sedimentary rocks occur in parts of Manitoba, Nunavut, Ontario, Quebec, the Maritime provinces, and Newfoundland and Labrador. However, these rocks are estimated to contain just two per cent of Canada's total conventional petroleum

resources. One area of Eastern Cratonic rock is the Michigan Basin that includes an area of southern Ontario and the adjacent Great Lakes. This area has been producing crude oil since the 1850s and natural gas since 1889. It continues to produce a small portion (less than one per cent) of Canada's current crude oil and natural gas supply.

Intermontane sedimentary rocks occur in the area of British Columbia and the Yukon located between the Canadian Rockies and the West Coast mountain ranges. There has been some oil and gas exploration in Intermontane areas, which are estimated to contain three per cent of Canada's total conventional petroleum resources. The Pacific Margin off the B.C. coast is estimated to contain four per cent of the nation's total conventional petroleum resources, but there has been no exploration since 1972 when the federal and provincial governments imposed moratoria on offshore drilling in the area. In 2001, the B.C. government initiated a review of its drilling ban, and a federal panel began hearings in 2004.

Did you know?

Most crude oil and natural gas originate from plant and animal life that thrived in oceans and lakes millions of years ago.

Despite neither review finding any scientific nor technological reason for maintaining the moratoria, provided a sound regulatory system was in place, they were not removed.

However, part of the B.C. Government's 2007 Energy Plan includes "ensuring offshore oil and gas resources are developed in a scientifically sound and environmentally responsible way."

Sedimentary basins span the U.S.-Canadian border between Alaska and Yukon, Montana and Alberta, North Dakota and Saskatchewan, North Dakota and Manitoba, Michigan and Ontario, and Maine and the Maritime provinces.

CROSS SECTION OF THE WESTERN CANADA SEDIMENTARY BASIN

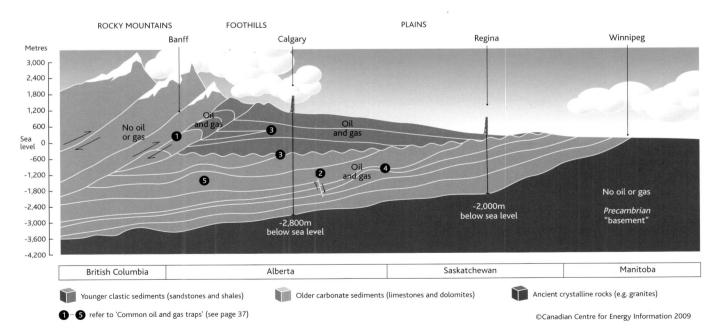

©Canadian Centre for Energy Information 2009

Formation of a sedimentary basin

Petroleum is most often found in a sedimentary basin. A sedimentary basin is a depressed area of the Earth's crust where tiny plants and animals lived or were deposited with mud and silt from streams and rivers. These sediments eventually hardened to form sedimentary rock. When exposed to heat and pressure over millions of years, the soft parts of plants and animals gradually changed to crude oil and natural gas. The temperature, pressure and compaction of sediments increase at greater depths.

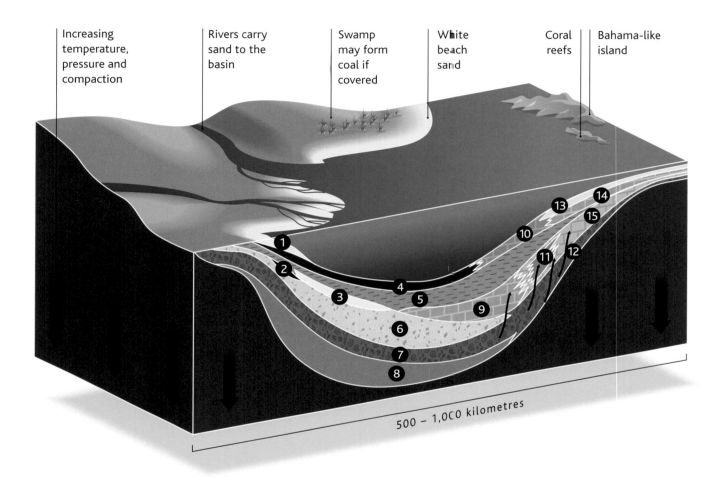

Increasing temperature, pressure and compaction

Rivers carry sand to the basin

Swamp may form coal if covered

White beach sand

Coral reefs

Bahama-like island

500 – 1,000 kilometres

❶ Delta sand
❷ Coal
❸ White sandstone (compacted beach sand)*
❹ Black mud settled from ocean water
❺ Shale formed by compaction of mud
❻ Brown sandstone (formed by compaction of river and delta sand)*
❼ Ancient shale (the heat down here turns organic matter into oil)
❽ Ancient sandstone*

❾ Limestone (compacted lime mud)*
❿ Lime mud washed offshore
⓫ Ancient reef*
⓬ Oil migrates from shale to the reef and forms an oil reservoir*
⓭ Lime, sand and shell debris
⓮ Limestone (rock) formed by compaction of lime sediment*
⓯ Dolomite formed by groundwater altering limestone*

* Potential future oil or gas reservoir

©Canadian Centre for Energy Information 2009

In the 1860s, hundreds of oil wells dotted the landscape around Petrolia, Ontario. The wooden derricks were left in place after drilling and were used to raise and lower tools needed to maintain the flow of oil from the wells.

Photo courtesy of Glenbow Archives NA-302-9

Black gold and blue flames

For thousands of years, people around the world noticed surface seeps of crude oil and natural gas, and occasionally used them for local heating and lighting. However, widespread commercial use did not begin until the 1850s when the growing scarcity and high cost of whale oil sparked a search for alternative lighting fuels. Canadians helped to usher in the new energy age.

Photo courtesy of BP Canada Energy Company

James Miller Williams, a carriage maker from Hamilton, Ontario, was the first man to bring in a commercial oil well in North America.

The first oil boom

Between 1846 and 1853, Abraham Gesner of Halifax, Nova Scotia, invented the process for making kerosene lamp fuel from coal. His method, called fractional distillation, was soon applied to "rock oil" from Pennsylvania and Ontario.

In 1850, geologist Thomas Sterry Hunt of the Geological Survey of Canada reported seepages of crude oil in the swampy "gum beds" of Enniskillen Township, Lambton County, Ontario. A year later, businessman Charles Tripp of Woodstock, Ontario, founded the International Mining and Manufacturing Company to exploit the asphalt beds and oil springs. Tripp also built the first asphalt production plant.

In 1855, Tripp sold his company to James Miller Williams. By 1858, Williams had dug a 15-metre well near Oil Springs, Ontario, that was producing significant quantities of crude oil. Williams' company transported the crude oil 200 kilometres to Hamilton, refined it there and sold lamp oil and other products. Since it was the first fully integrated petroleum company in North America, Williams is often called the founding father of Canada's petroleum industry.

Petrolia became a boom town in the 1860s and 1870s as hundreds of wells were sunk in the area and about 18 small, primitive refineries converted the crude oil into lamp fuel, paraffin, grease, lubricating oil and asphalt.

Gasoline was discarded as waste until the internal combustion engine was commercialized near the end of the century. Sixteen Ontario producing and refining companies merged in 1880 to form the Imperial Oil Company Limited.

The search for new crude oil supplies

As the 20th century dawned, the spread of electric lighting reduced demand for lamp fuel at the same time that Ontario's crude oil production dwindled. Within a few years, however, huge new markets emerged for refined oil products – especially gasoline for automobiles and fuel oil for naval ships. Soon fuel would also be needed for airplanes, military vehicles, tractors, trucks and more. During the first half of the century, imports from the United States and Latin America supplied up to 90 per cent of Canada's crude oil requirements.

The search for new crude oil supplies eventually spread to every corner of Canada. The huge hydrocarbon resources of Alberta's oil sands had long been known, and attracted attention of the Geological Survey of Canada as early as 1875. However, it took a half-century before Karl Clark invented a

Photo courtesy of Syncrude Canada Ltd.

Pioneer scientist Karl Clark of the Alberta Research Council developed a method for separating bitumen from sand. This process was key to the eventual development of large-scale oil sands mining projects.

Geological Survey of Canada

The Geological Survey of Canada (GSC) was established in 1842. It was Canada's first scientific agency, and one of the nation's first government organizations of any kind. The GSC's initial focus was to look for coal and other minerals. Throughout its long history, the GSC has played a key role in gathering, recording and analyzing basic information about Canada's natural resources and other important aspects of the nation's geology.

method of separating bitumen from sand in 1925 and nearly as long again before the first commercially successful large-scale oil sands plant began operating near Fort McMurray in 1967.

Until 1947, there were only a few significant conventional oil developments outside Ontario. Three rounds of discoveries near Turner Valley, Alberta, beginning in 1914, provided crude oil for nearby markets and helped establish Calgary as the head-office city of the Canadian oil and gas industry. Heavy crude oil was discovered near Wainwright, Alberta, in 1923, and was used to make asphalt for paving and roofing. Discovered in 1920, the oilfield at Norman Wells in the Northwest Territories supplied oil products to nearby settlements and enjoyed a brief stardom during the Second World War when an expensive pipeline temporarily linked it to Whitehorse, Yukon, and Fairbanks, Alaska.

The turning point

The turning point for the industry occurred on February 13, 1947, when Imperial Oil unveiled a large crude oil discovery near Leduc, Alberta, after failing to find a major new oilfield while drilling 133 exploratory wells across Western Canada in the previous 14 years. Leduc was the first major Canadian crude oil discovery based on a seismic survey, and it led to a series of other discoveries in the area. By 1953, pipelines connected the Alberta oilfields to markets in Ontario, British Columbia, and the Prairies.

Encouraged by the Leduc success, which altered theories about the region's geology, companies used seismic surveys and other new exploration technologies to make a series of stunning discoveries in Western Canada: Daly, Manitoba, in 1951; Midale, Saskatchewan, and Pembina, Alberta, in 1953; Swan Hills, Alberta, and Clarke Lake, British Columbia, in 1957; Rainbow Lake, Alberta, in 1965; and West Pembina, Alberta, in 1977.

Photo courtesy of Provincial Archives of Alberta

Natural gas for Canadians

The leading pioneer of the early Canadian natural gas industry was Eugene Coste, who developed wells and distribution pipelines in southwestern Ontario from 1889 to 1904 and then moved to Alberta where he built Canada's first long-distance natural gas pipeline, 270 kilometres from Bow Island to Calgary. Natural gas had first been discovered in eastern Alberta in 1883, and since 1890 residents of Medicine Hat had been using gas found beneath the town for cooking, heating and lighting. Edmonton initiated natural gas service in 1923, but the early gas systems in most other Canadian cities distributed coal gas, a mixture of carbon monoxide, methane and hydrogen, obtained by heating coal in a closed vessel.

Large reservoirs of natural gas were discovered in Alberta in the 1940s and in British Columbia and Saskatchewan in the 1950s. Pipelines shipped western Canadian natural gas to Vancouver consumers in 1957 and to Ontario and Quebec in 1958. Political controversy over the pipelines led to the establishment of the National Energy Board in 1959 to

Photo courtesy of BP Canada Energy Company

Leduc Discovery (top)
On February 13, 1947, Imperial Oil unveiled a major crude oil discovery near Leduc, Alberta. Within a year, a major boom was underway in Western Canada.

Drillers on the Leduc rig
Success of the Leduc well created opportunities for thousands of oil workers, many of them returning to civilian life after military service. The influx threatened to overwhelm the small town of Leduc, so Imperial Oil helped to build a new community, Devon, just north of the #1 well, to house its workers. A roughneck on a rig in 1947 earned about 90 cents an hour, equivalent to $10.15 in 2007. No special training was required, and many young Albertans went directly from the farm to the rig.

Photo courtesy of Enbridge Inc.

The longest crude oil pipeline in the world
The Interprovincial crude oil pipeline (now part of Enbridge Inc.) was built between Edmonton, Alberta, and Superior, Wisconsin in 1950, and extended to Sarnia, Ontario in 1953. Later additions connected the system to refineries in Chicago and Montreal and as far south as Wood River in southern Illinois. Another branch of the pipeline, completed in 1985, extends to the oil field at Norman Wells in the Northwest Territories. The Enbridge system was – and remains – the world's longest crude oil pipeline network.

oversee interprovincial and international energy trade in Canada. In 1938, Alberta had already established the first provincial regulatory authority to manage resource development – now known as the Alberta Energy Resources Conservation Board.

Photo courtesy of Glenbow Archives NA-1446-24

Eugene Coste, an entrepreneur from southwestern Ontario, was the first Canadian to find and develop natural gas resources on a large scale.

Frontiers and crises

As the consumption of crude oil and natural gas soared in the 1960s and 1970s, the number of large discoveries in Western Canada declined. Companies extended seismic and drilling programs to the Arctic and to waters off Canada's Atlantic, Pacific and Arctic coasts. These efforts eventually led to large crude oil discoveries on the Grand Banks off Newfoundland and Labrador – beginning with the Hibernia field in 1979 – as well as significant crude oil and natural gas off Nova Scotia, natural gas in the Mackenzie Delta and the Arctic Islands, and crude oil in the Beaufort Sea.

On Canada's other "frontier" – unlocking the sticky wealth of the Alberta oil sands – a second large mining project was built in the 1970s, and several other projects used steam recovery to separate bitumen from sand within deeper underground deposits. Improvements in oil sands

recovery technologies during the 1980s and 1990s reduced costs to levels more competitive with conventional crude oil production and led to large investment commitments in new and existing projects in the late 1990s.

Two international crises – the Arab oil embargo in 1973 and the Iranian revolution in 1978 and 1979 – caused sharp increases in crude oil prices and led to a re-examination of energy policies. In Canada, as a consequence, governments became much more involved in the oil and gas industry, culminating in the federal government's National Energy Program in 1980. Many of the regulatory policies and market restrictions were reversed or relaxed in the mid-1980s. The long-term effects of escalating oil prices brought on by these crises included trends toward more fuel-efficient motor vehicles, better-insulated buildings, and a widespread switch from crude oil to natural gas for heating, industrial processes and electricity generation.

Legacies

The legacies of the oil and gas industry's long history in Canada include:

- a vast body of knowledge about the nation's geology and petroleum resources, available to all industry participants through federal and provincial reporting requirements and databases
- highly skilled professional and technical personnel, many with international experience
- extensive experience with challenging resources (sour gas, heavy oil, oil sands) and with challenging environments such as the Arctic and offshore
- an infrastructure of plants, pipelines and facilities supporting and linking every aspect of a far-reaching industry
- training and educational institutions to prepare workers and specialists for the industry's needs
- laws, policies and regulatory authorities to ensure the industry operates in the public interest.

However, past practices also led to impacts on land, air and water resources and affected plants, animals and humans. As scientific knowledge expanded and society's expectations increased, government and industry continually raised performance standards and attempted to address the effects of earlier activities. Similarly, there was an ongoing improvement in measures to protect the health and safety of workers and nearby residents.

In the rest of this book, readers will learn about the ways science and technology are used today to find, produce, process, deliver and utilize crude oil and natural gas, as well as the challenges we are facing in developing and using these resources.

Technologies

A floating production, storage and offloading vessel extracts crude oil from the Terra Nova field off Newfoundland and Labrador. Giant trucks are replacing bucketwheels and conveyors in Alberta oil sands mining operations.

Photo courtesy of Syncrude Canada Ltd.

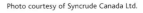

Photo courtesy of Petro-Canada

Learn More

The Centre for Energy's *Evolution of Canada's Oil and Gas Industry* describes the industry's trial-and-error pioneering start in the 1850s to the advanced science and technology of the 21st century. Free to download at **www.centreforenergy.com/Education/Bookstore**

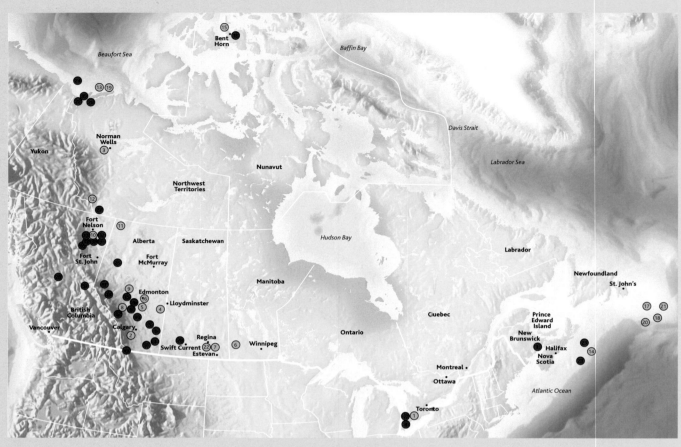

©Canadian Centre for Energy Information 2009

Crude oil and natural gas discoveries

Crude Oil (green)

1.	1851	Petrolia, Ont.
2.	1914	Turner Valley, Alta.
3.	1920	Norman Wells, N.W.T.
4.	1923	Wainwright, Alta.
	1924	Turner Valley, Alta.
5.	1947	Leduc, Alta.
6.	1951	Daly, Man.
7.	1953	Midale, Sask.
8.	1953	Pembina, Alta.
9.	1957	Swan Hills, Alta.
10.	1957	Clarke Lake, B.C.
11.	1965	Rainbow Lake, Alta.
12.	1966	Pointed Mountain, N.W.T.
13.	1969	Atkinson Point, N.W.T.
14.	1973	Panuke-Cohasset, N.S.
15.	1973	Bent Horn, Cameron Island
16.	1977	West Pembina, Alta.
17.	1979	Hibernia, Nfld.
18.	1981	Hebron-Ben Nevis, Nfld.
19.	1984	Amauligak, N.W.T.
20.	1985	Terra Nova, Nfld.
21.	1985	White Rose, Nfld.
22.	2004	Bakken, Sask.

Natural Gas (red)

1.	1859	New Brunswick
2.	1866	Southwestern Ontario
3.	1883	Medicine Hat, Alta.
4.	1889	Essex County, Ont.
5.	1904	Cessford, Alta.
6.	1904	Suffield, Alta.
7.	1909	Bow Island, Alta.
8.	1954	Westerose South, Alta.
9.	1955	Elmworth, Alta.
10.	1956	Crossfield, Alta.
11.	1956	Clarke Lake, B.C.
12.	1959	Brazeau River, Alta.
13.	1959	Waterton, Alta.
14.	1961	Kaybob South, Alta.
15.	1962	Edson, Alta.
16.	1962	Yoyo, B.C.
17.	1965	Sierra, B.C.
18.	1969	Drake Point, Nunavut.
19.	1971	Taglu, N.W.T.
20.	1972	Parson's Lake, N.W.T.
21.	1972	Thebaud, N.S.
22.	1973	Niglintgak, N.W.T.
23.	1979	Venture, N.S.
24.	1980	Issungnak, N.W.T.
25.	1983	Hamburg, Alta.
26.	1986	Caroline, Alta.
27.	1997	Fort Liard, N.W.T.
28.	1999	Shackleton, Sask.
29.	2000	Ladyfern, B.C.
30.	2002	Greater Sierra, B.C.
31.	2002	Monkman, B.C.
32.	2005	Horn River, B.C.
33.	2005	Montney, B.C.

The lifeblood of modern Canadian society

Crude oil and natural gas provide 70 per cent of the energy consumed by Canadians, but these substances have become so central to modern life in our offices, classrooms and homes that it is easy to take them for granted. Here are just a few everyday products and uses:

- computers, cell phones, televisions, ipods – many plastic components made from crude oil and natural gas
- heat – natural gas or fuel oil for the furnace
- hot water – natural gas for the water heater
- electricity – may be generated from natural gas or, in some areas, diesel fuel
- traffic outside – gasoline and diesel fuel for vehicles but also lubricants, antifreeze, synthetic rubber tires, plastic components, fibres and resins in composite materials, paint, shatter-proof glass, even the asphalt pavement

- airplanes flying overhead – aviation fuel, lubricants, plastic components, composite materials, asphalt runways
- furniture – glues in wood composites, plastic parts, fabrics
- carpet – synthetic fibres and backing materials
- lunch – bags, films and packaging, with food grown using diesel-powered tractors and fertilizers made from natural gas
- medicines, cosmetics and clothing – all made from petroleum products, and
- how it all got here – the vast network of road, rail, air and water transportation systems, relying on fuels from refined petroleum products.

The industry that makes these goods and services possible comprises many kinds of businesses, from those that explore for petroleum to those that sell natural gas and refined oil products to the consumer. The oil and gas industry provides a significant market to many other industries that produce the goods and services – such as steel, motor vehicles, engineering and computer systems – that are used in its operations. Employment and spending are spread throughout the economy and across the country. The direct and indirect income generated from crude oil and natural gas production contributes significantly to the national economy. In addition, the industry pays taxes and royalties that boost government revenues at all levels.

**CANADIAN PRIMARY ENERGY DEMAND BY FUEL
(thousands of petajoules)**

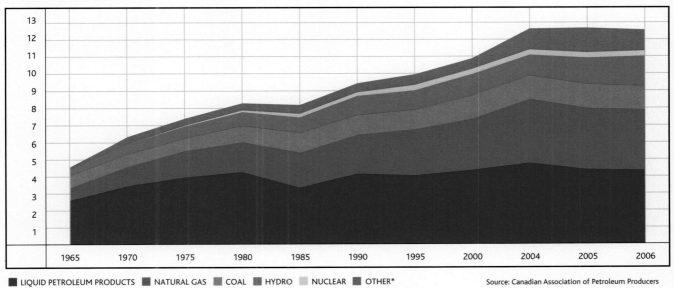

■ LIQUID PETROLEUM PRODUCTS ■ NATURAL GAS ■ COAL ■ HYDRO ■ NUCLEAR ■ OTHER*

Source: Canadian Association of Petroleum Producers

* Includes biomass and wind

A versatile source of energy and products

Natural gas heats homes and businesses in much of the country, from Vancouver Island to Quebec City to Inuvik, and natural gas distribution is being developed in the Maritimes. Heating oil and propane are also important residential and commercial fuels, especially in areas not served by natural gas.

Mobility is crucial for the widely dispersed Canadian population. Asphalt for road paving is obtained from petroleum, while oil products such as gasoline, diesel and jet fuel provide the energy for virtually all our transportation systems – road, off-road, rail, air and water. Even bicycles and electric-powered urban transit vehicles depend on oil products for their lubrication and manufacture. The synthetic rubber and nylon in tires, for example, are manufactured from petroleum.

Crude oil and natural gas help supply Canadians with food. Agricultural machinery runs on oil products, as do the trucks and railways that transport food from farm to supermarket. A number of fertilizers are made from natural gas and from sulphur, a byproduct of natural gas production. Crude oil and natural gas are also used in the manufacture of herbicides and pesticides.

The many uses of natural gas

Versatility is the hallmark of natural gas. In Canada, it is the leading source of heat for homes and businesses. Generating electricity from natural gas is one of the fastest-growing uses of this clean-burning fuel. Natural gas also provides about 26 per cent of the energy used for manufacturing in Canada. It is vitally important in making cement, processing forest products and manufacturing steel. Natural gas is a key raw material in the fertilizer and petrochemical industries and provides energy and hydrogen for the production of synthetic crude oil from oil sands bitumen.

Natural gas liquids – ethane, propane, butane and condensates (pentanes and heavier hydrocarbons) produced along with natural gas – are used as fuels for heating and motor vehicles, and are a primary source of feedstocks for petrochemicals and oil refining.

COMPONENTS OF RAW NATURAL GAS

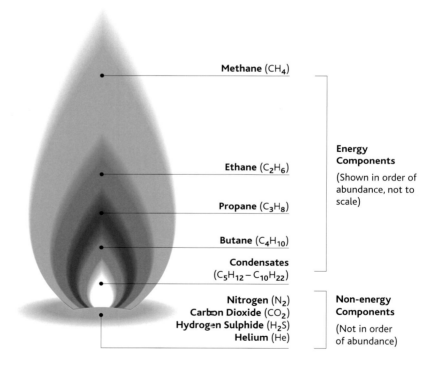

Methane (CH_4)

Ethane (C_2H_6)

Propane (C_3H_8)

Butane (C_4H_{10})

Condensates ($C_5H_{12} - C_{10}H_{22}$)

Energy Components
(Shown in order of abundance, not to scale)

Nitrogen (N_2)
Carbon Dioxide (CO_2)
Hydrogen Sulphide (H_2S)
Helium (He)

Non-energy Components
(Not in order of abundance)

©Canadian Centre for Energy Information 2009

Petroleum products in our daily lives

Crude oil is a mixture of many thousands of molecules, each with particular physical and chemical properties. Hundreds of products are made by separating and sorting these molecules, then re-combining or further processing them.

The range of products varies according to the particular type of crude oil and the refinery design. Processes can be altered to produce more gasoline in summer or more heating oil in winter.

On average, processing light crude oil in a modern refinery yields the following range of products:

- **Gasoline** to fuel cars, motorcycles, light trucks, small planes, boats, off-road vehicles, snowmobiles, lawn mowers, chainsaws, leaf and snow blowers, emergency generators, camp stoves, etc. (about 40 per cent of the original crude oil volume)

- **Diesel fuel** for some cars, most trucks and buses, railway locomotives, construction and forestry equipment, farm tractors, many boats and ships, larger electric generators, etc. (25 per cent)

- **Light fuel oil** for heating homes and buildings, many industrial processes, and the fuel for some ships (8 per cent)

- **Other products** including asphalt for road paving and roofing, lubricants such as motor oil and grease, waxes for candles and polishes, and the raw materials for petrochemicals such as polystyrene and synthetic rubber (10 per cent)

- **Heavy fuel oil** for electric power generation, large ships and some industrial processes (8 per cent)

- **Aviation jet fuel** for airplanes and helicopters (5 per cent)

- The **refining process** itself consumes crude oil or an equivalent amount of energy from other sources such as natural gas (4 per cent)

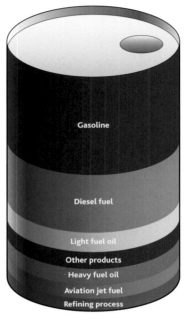

Gasoline

Diesel fuel

Light fuel oil

Other products

Heavy fuel oil

Aviation jet fuel

Refining process

©Canadian Centre for Energy Information 2009

Products made with petroleum can be found in every part of the typical Canadian home

In the structure itself:
- Styrofoam® insulation
- polyethylene vapour barriers
- glues in plywood and panelboard
- insulation on wiring
- shingles and caulking
- plastic pipes

In the kitchen and bathroom:
- plastic containers
- cleansers
- plastic utensils
- seals and insulation
- tiles and countertops
- toothbrushes
- combs and brushes
- pharmaceuticals
- fuel for gas stoves

In the bedrooms and closets:
- synthetic fibres in clothing and bedding
- glues and parts in furniture
- plastics in wall fixtures

In the living room and den:
- plastic components in electronic appliances
- synthetic fibres in carpets and floor coverings
- glues and parts in furniture

In the furnace and laundry room:
- heating oil or natural gas for heat
- natural gas for hot water tanks and clothes dryers
- plastic pipes and fittings

In the garage:
- lubricants and fuel for vehicles, lawn mowers and snow blowers
- plastic garden tools and lawn furniture
- paints, pesticides and fertilizers
- asphalt driveway pavement
- plastic components in vehicles

Photos courtesy of ConocoPhillips

Creating wealth and employment

The oil and gas industry is a significant source of employment in every province – in ways that range from developing new supplies of energy to operating retail outlets. The industry directly and indirectly employs more than half a million Canadians.

In Canada, the revenues generated by finding, producing, processing, transporting, refining and selling petroleum contribute to our relatively high standard of living.

Through taxes, royalties and other payments to government, the petroleum industry is a major contributor to health care, education and social programs. From 2000 to 2007, the industry paid an average $19.2 billion annually to governments.

The industry plays a particularly visible role in those towns and cities that are located in or near petroleum exploration and production such as St. John's,

Newfoundland and Labrador, Fort St. John, British Columbia, Inuvik, Northwest Territories, and Fort McMurray, Alberta. Similarly, oil refining is central to cities such as Saint John, New Brunswick, and Sarnia, Ontario, and plays a big role in the economies of Montreal and Edmonton.

The effect on employment, economic development and government revenues can be seen clearly in Newfoundland and Labrador and Nova Scotia, where crude oil and natural gas production is a recent development. The Conference Board of Canada has estimated that oil and gas development could generate between 25,000 and 90,000 additional jobs in Nova Scotia over the next two decades, depending on how much petroleum is found off the province's shores. Another study indicated that the direct and indirect effects of the Hibernia crude oil project off Newfoundland and Labrador added 3,100 jobs to the province's economy,

reduced unemployment by 1.6 per cent and increased personal income by $168 million. The effects of offshore development on the economic activity and government finances of the two provinces are already significant and could be even more dramatic in the future.

The rapid growth of Fort McMurray as the centre of the oil sands industry is another example. Between 2000 and 2007, Fort McMurray's population increased 55 per cent from 42,156 to 65,400. In many rural, remote and Aboriginal communities, the petroleum industry is a leading source of employment, training, business opportunities and local government revenues.

The oil and gas industry is equally vital to the entire Canadian economy. It provides products and services to meet people's needs and generates revenue for governments, investors, employees and the communities in which they live and work.

The Canadian industry's role in the world

Canada is the world's third largest natural gas-producing nation and the largest supplier of U.S. natural gas imports. Crude oil production is ample for the nation's needs, but small by comparison to that of Russia or Saudi Arabia or even our main customer to the south, the United States. Simply stated, Canadian production is a relatively small factor in the world crude oil industry, although it is important in North America.

Canada is one of the four largest suppliers of U.S. crude oil imports, along with Saudi Arabia, Mexico and Venezuela. Canada's crude oil exports are partly offset by imports of smaller volumes of crude oil and refined oil products, mainly into markets east of Sarnia, Ontario. Most of the Canadian imports come from the North Sea, South America, the Middle East and Africa. According to

Statistics Canada, crude oil and natural gas contributed $60.3 billion to Canada's trade balance in 2008.

Domestic crude oil and natural gas production gives Canada a competitive advantage among industrial nations. The European Union, for example, currently imports more than 70 per cent of its crude oil and more than 50 per cent of its natural gas.

In terms of total hydrocarbon resources, Canada has great potential. A great deal of conventional crude oil and natural gas remains in the Western Canada Sedimentary Basin. Other resources include crude oil and natural gas in the Arctic and off the East Coast as well as bitumen from the Alberta oil sands, heavy oil in Alberta and Saskatchewan, and natural gas from coal seams (coalbed methane). Additional petroleum resources are believed to lie off the West Coast. The rate at which all these resources are developed depends mainly on four

related factors: technology, access to resources, environmental effects, and production costs relative to market price. Canadian companies are significant players on the world stage, and Canadian expertise is widely sought. One example is the success of Canadians in extinguishing oil fires in Kuwait after the 1991 Gulf War. Many other countries send their oil and gas personnel to Canada for education, training and work experience.

Canadian companies and specialized workers also play an important role in developing other countries' crude oil and natural gas resources. Canadian skills, knowledge, equipment, systems and capital can be found in exploration, production and transportation projects around the world. In 2006, according to a survey by *Doig's Digest*, 47 Canadian companies produced a total of 124,100 cubic metres per day of crude oil and liquids in 32 foreign countries; 35 companies produced 68 million cubic metres per day of natural gas in 22 foreign counties.

TOTAL VALUE OF CANADIAN EXPORTS

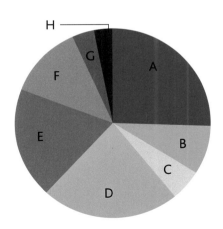

	$ billions	%
A Energy Products	126	25.7
B Agriculture and Fishing Products	41	8.4
C Forestry Products	26	5.3
D Industrial Goods and Materials	111	22.7
E Machinery and Equipment	93	19.0
F Automotive Products	61	12.4
G Other Consumer Goods	18	3.7
H Unallocated Adjustments	14	2.8
Total	490	100.0

VALUE OF CANADIAN ENERGY EXPORTS

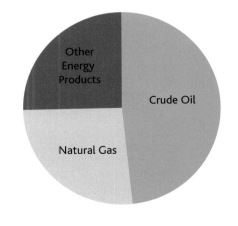

	$ millions	%
Crude Oil	60,975	48.4
Natural Gas	33,296	26.4
*Other Energy Products	31,795	25.2
Total	126,066	100.0

Source: Statistics Canada 2008
*Includes gasoline, other refined products, electricity, coal and natural gas liquids.

Careers in energy

Employment in the petroleum industry includes jobs commonly associated with the oil and gas industry – geologists, geophysicists, engineers, land agents, seismic crews, drillers, drilling mud specialists, oil sands mining workers, plant operators and the like – and hundreds of other supply, service and support positions. Examples include truckers, safety and environmental protection personnel, chefs, service boat crews, helicopter and airplane pilots, rig fabricators, landscapers, even archeologists.

Learn more about careers in energy at **www.centreforenergy.com**

Three main components of the industry

Photo courtesy of Tesco Corporation

The upstream sector

The Canadian upstream sector includes more than 1,000 exploration and production companies as well as hundreds of associated businesses such as seismic and drilling contractors, service rig operators, engineering firms and various scientific, technical, service and supply companies.

The midstream sector

The midstream sector consists of pipeline systems that connect producing and consuming areas. Other midstream facilities extract sulphur and natural gas liquids, store oil and gas products and transport products by truck, rail or tanker.

The downstream sector

The downstream sector consists of refineries, petrochemical companies, natural gas distribution utilities, refined oil product wholesalers and retail sites.

Photo courtesy of Syncrude Canada Ltd.

Leading-edge tools and knowledge

In terms of tools and knowledge, the Canadian oil and gas industry is a world leader in many fields:

- high-tech exploration and enhanced-recovery production methods
- cold-climate operations
- harsh-environment offshore development
- development of oil sands and sour gas resources
- gas processing, sulphur extraction and heavy oil upgrading
- construction and operation of pipelines
- specialized controls and computer applications
- safety and environmental protection technology and training
- consultation with stakeholders
- government regulation
- historical data sources, now computerized, and information sharing
- innovative products and services that meet customer needs, and
- refining processes that produce quality petroleum-based products while reducing the impact on the environment.

The difference between heavy and light oil

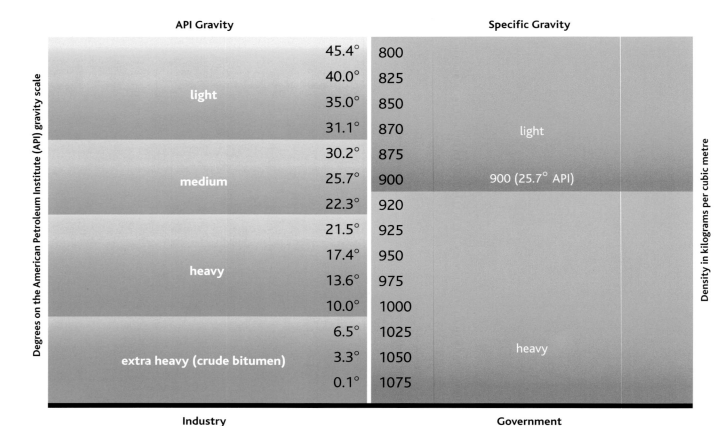

API Gravity

Specific Gravity

Degrees on the American Petroleum Institute (API) gravity scale

Density in kilograms per cubic metre

API	Specific Gravity
45.4°	800
40.0°	825
35.0°	850
31.1°	870
30.2°	875
25.7°	900
22.3°	920
21.5°	925
17.4°	950
13.6°	975
10.0°	1000
6.5°	1025
3.3°	1050
0.1°	1075

light

medium

heavy

extra heavy (crude bitumen)

light

900 (25.7° API)

heavy

Industry

Government

©Canadian Centre for Energy Information 2009

Light crude oil contains many small, hydrogen-rich hydrocarbon molecules. Light oil flows easily through wells and pipelines. When light oil is refined, it produces a large quantity of transportation fuels such as gasoline, diesel and jet fuel. Light oil commands the highest price per barrel.

Heavy crude oil contains many large, carbon-rich hydrocarbon molecules. Additional pumping is needed to make heavy oil flow through wells and pipelines. Heavy crude oil contains a smaller proportion of natural gasoline and diesel fuel components and requires much more extensive refining

to make transportation fuels. Heavy oil commands a lower price and the difference in price per barrel is called the differential.

Synthetic crude oil is a hydrocarbon liquid produced by upgrading conventional heavy oil or bitumen extracted from oil sands. The mixture consists of hydrocarbons derived from heavy crude oil or bitumen through the addition of hydrogen and/or the removal of carbon. Synthetic crude oil sells at a premium price compared to most other crude oils.

The "weight" of different crude oils can be measured on either the metric density scale (kilograms per cubic metre) or the American Petroleum Institute gravity scale (°API). Government authorities in Canada only distinguish between "heavy" and "light" crude oil types, while various other definitions are used by the industry. The illustration shows definitions suggested by the Petroleum Society of the Canadian Institute of Mining and Metallurgy.

How the business works

Revenues of the Canadian upstream oil and gas industry were estimated at $110.5 billion in 2007, according to the Canadian Association of Petroleum Producers. A little more than half of this amount came from the sale of crude oil while the remainder was from natural gas, natural gas liquids and sulphur. Most of the revenues were spent in three major areas:

- exploration and development of new supplies
- production costs for existing fields, and
- taxes and other payments to governments and landowners.

In 2007, $13.6 billion was collected by the industry on behalf of federal and provincial governments in the form of taxes. Gasoline, the main downstream product, accounted for about 42 per cent of refined oil product sales. Canadian consumers paid a total of about $23 billion for natural gas in 2007.

From drilling rig to retail site, the petroleum industry directly and indirectly employed about 375,000 Canadians in 2007. Total employment impact, including steelmakers, accountants, couriers and others reached 500,000.

The public interest

Federal, provincial, regional and local authorities regulate operations of the oil and gas industry in Canada. The majority of Canadian oil and gas resources are found on federal or provincial Crown lands, and the Crown owns the mineral rights for more than 80 per cent of the underground formations believed to contain crude oil or natural gas. Governments therefore have a direct ownership role as well as a broader responsibility to make sure the industry operates in the public interest. Royalties are payments for the "owner's share" of production. Royalties are an important source of government revenue in petroleum-producing areas. Through legislation and regulatory authorities, governments also create a framework for negotiating access to lands where the landowners do not own the mineral rights.

The National Energy Board regulates interprovincial and international energy trade, including pipelines carrying crude oil and natural gas, and assists territorial governments in regulating exploration and development of oil and natural gas. The Canada-Newfoundland and Labrador Offshore Petroleum Board and the Canada-Nova Scotia Offshore Petroleum Board regulate East Coast offshore activity on behalf of the federal and provincial governments. Provincial authorities such as the Alberta Utilities Commission, the Alberta Energy Resources Conservation Board and the B.C. Oil and Gas Commission regulate development within their jurisdictions.

Provincial and territorial authorities establish regulations for activities such as oil refining, fuel retailing and local natural gas distribution.

VALUE OF UPSTREAM PRODUCTION AND PAYMENTS TO GOVERNMENTS ($ billions)

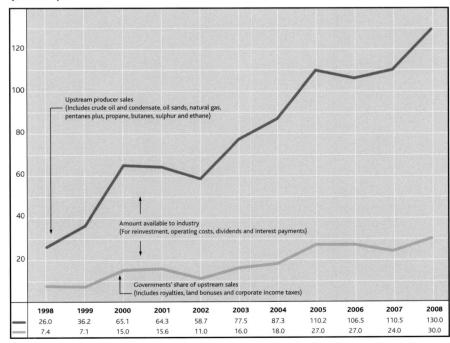

	1998	1999	2000	2001	2002	2003	2004	2005	2006	2007	2008
	26.0	36.2	65.1	64.3	58.7	77.5	87.3	110.2	106.5	110.5	130.0
	7.4	7.1	15.0	15.6	11.0	16.0	18.0	27.0	27.0	24.0	30.0

©Canadian Association of Petroleum Producers

Photo courtesy of Petro-Canada

Petroleum prices

In Canada, competitive market forces determine the prices of crude oil, natural gas and most refined oil products. The exceptions are gasoline prices in Prince Edward Island, Nova Scotia, New Brunswick, Quebec and Newfoundland and Labrador, which are regulated by provincial authorities in various manners.

Because transporting crude oil by ocean is relatively inexpensive, the prices of various types of crude oil are more or less uniform around the world. Prices move up and down on a daily or even hourly basis according to perceptions of global supply and demand. The Organization of Petroleum Exporting Countries (OPEC) continues to influence world crude oil prices by setting production targets for members. However, due to growing production in non-OPEC countries such as Russia, Norway, the United Kingdom, Canada, Brazil, Argentina, and China, the organization no longer has the same degree of control in the international oil market that it did in the 1970s and early 1980s. OPEC comprises 12 oil-exporting countries (Algeria, Angola, Ecuador, Iran, Iraq, Kuwait, Libya, Nigeria, Qatar, Saudi Arabia, United Arab Emirates, and Venezuela) that together produce about 40 per cent of world crude oil.

The natural gas challenge

Canada's annual natural gas production increased almost 20 per cent between 1995 and 2001. During that time Canadian natural gas satisfied continuing growth in domestic markets while increasing exports to the United States by almost a third. In 2002, the record of growth came to an end, as the number of new natural gas wells fell by 17 per cent and overall production began to level off. Despite higher prices and substantial increases in drilling from 2003 to 2006, supply growth remained flat. Does this mean the limit has been reached for conventional gas production from Western Canada? What does the future hold for alternative sources of Canadian natural gas?

A study by the Canadian Energy Research Institute in 2003 attempted to answer these questions. The study examined several possible scenarios for future natural gas supplies and concluded that "so long as supplies of gas from unconventional sources such as coal-bed methane and from new basins can be brought on stream in a timely manner, natural gas production in Canada can be sustained at significant levels." The analysis found, however, that maintaining or increasing production would probably involve ever-increasing costs to find and produce new natural gas supplies.

HISTORICAL CRUDE OIL PRICES
($ U.S. per barrel)

($ U.S. per cubic metre)

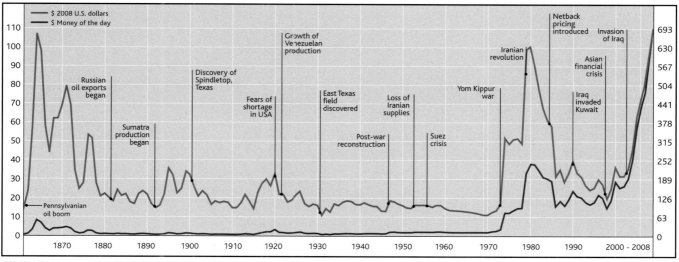

1861-1944 U.S. average   1945-1983 Arabian light posted at Ras Tanura   1984-2008 Brent dated

Source: BP Statistical Review of World Energy

The price of natural gas in Canada is determined by forces in the continental North American market. The factors that influence natural gas pricing are similar to those affecting crude oil prices, and include:

- the distance between markets and producing areas
- transportation charges
- the availability of pipeline capacity
- the amount of natural gas in storage
- the volume of purchases
- the cost of competing energy sources such as fuel oil
- regional demand changes due to weather extremes, and
- the overall balance between continental supply and demand.

The United States imports a small amount of liquefied natural gas by tanker from abroad, but in the past the cost of transportation and facilities has generally made liquefied natural gas too costly to be competitive in the North American market. In the future, higher natural gas prices are expected to encourage additional liquefied natural gas imports into North America.

Provincial governments regulate the rates charged by local distribution companies for delivering natural gas to end users. However, governments generally allow market pricing of the energy component of consumers' natural gas bills. In some provinces, beginning with Ontario in 1998, independent marketers are allowed to sell natural gas directly to end users. These independent marketers compete with the marketing arms of local distribution companies. The natural gas is still delivered in the same pipelines, but the consumer may pay the energy component to the marketer and only the delivery rate to the distribution company.

HISTORICAL WESTERN CANADIAN NATURAL GAS PRICES
($ Cdn per thousand cubic feet)

($ Cdn per thousand cubic metres)

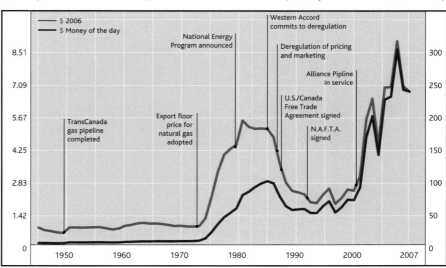

Source: Canadian Association of Petroleum Producers

How prices affect employment

Photo courtesy of Suncor Energy

In the mid-1980s, supplies of crude oil and natural gas exceeded the demand for these commodities in world and North American markets. This led to a sharp reduction in prices, which cut into profits and forced the Canadian industry to improve its efficiency and productivity. Employment in the upstream industry declined more than 25 per cent between 1985 and 1992, although the volume of crude oil and natural gas production increased.

The industry's health improved considerably in the mid-1990s as commodity prices recovered. More pipelines were built to Canadian and U.S. markets, and exports of Canadian crude oil and natural gas increased. The additional sales helped to generate the profits that are essential to attract the people and capital needed to ensure the industry's future. With renewed confidence came new investments in East Coast offshore oil and gas projects, the Alberta oil sands, and natural gas exploration and development in Western Canada. Although a 30 per cent drop in crude oil prices slowed industry activity in 1998, major projects continued to go

ahead and picked up speed when crude oil prices rose 57 per cent and natural gas prices rose 86 per cent in 2000. Oil prices continued to rise, peaking at $147 per barrel in July 2008, before falling back to below $40 per barrel in early 2009 then rebounding. Natural gas prices peaked in 2005, fell back for two years, rebounded in early 2008, then fell sharply.

The composition of the upstream oil and gas industry also changed considerably in the past decade. The larger companies grew even larger through mergers, acquisitions and their own successes. They needed to be very big to pursue major investments such as international exploration, offshore development and oil sands projects. Consequently, many mid-sized companies were acquired during this restructuring. Smaller companies sought out specialized niches – such as shallow natural gas or low-productivity oil wells in Western Canada – where they could develop local expertise and operate cost-efficiently.

As well, petroleum royalty trusts gained popularity in the 1990s. A petroleum royalty trust is an investment vehicle

that provides income to its unitholders from the revenues of oil and gas producing properties. Unlike traditional oil and gas companies, trusts distribute their cash flow to their unit holders, and consequently do not reserve funds for exploration. The popularity of royalty trusts drew investment away from medium-sized companies until 2007 when the tax advantage was dropped effective in 2011.

Downstream employment fell sharply in the early 1990s but has risen slowly since 1996. The outlook for the downstream sector depends on its ability to compete with imports of refined products, the demand for refined products in Canada, and the effects of meeting new environmental standards. Less efficient refineries have been shut down over the past 20 years (the last new Canadian refinery was built in Alberta in 1984. One Alberta refinery has suspended operations since 2001, and another in Ontario closed in 2005). The remaining facilities are generally large and efficient. Competition at the retail pumps continues to be intense. Despite many service station closures, the number of retail outlets per capita in many markets is still higher than in the United States. When there are too many outlets, each station pumps less gasoline and its operating costs per litre are therefore higher.

Consumer demand for natural gas and refined petroleum products increased in Canada and the United States during the 1990s due to population and economic growth, a trend to larger vehicles and more driving, and greater use of natural gas to generate electricity. Meeting these demands will require continuing advances in efficiency, productivity and innovation. New employment opportunities will undoubtedly emerge in many sectors.

Photo courtesy of ConocoPhillips

Reserves and resources

In the long term, the key factor for the industry and the economy is the amount of crude oil and natural gas in the ground. These buried hydrocarbons are called resources and include all the natural gas, bitumen, crude oil and natural gas liquids contained in Canada.

The National Energy Board (NEB) collects information from provincial and territorial authorities to prepare national estimates of resources. The NEB has estimated that Canada's original resources include 58 billion cubic metres of recoverable crude oil and bitumen and approximately 14 trillion cubic metres of recoverable natural gas. More than 90 per cent of Canada's oil resources are oil sands bitumen of which about 12 per cent is recoverable with existing technology, while almost half of the natural gas resources are located in Arctic and offshore areas.

Only a fraction of the resources in place can be produced economically with existing technology at any given time. To provide consistent standards of measurement, companies and governments have developed various ways of calculating reserves, which are the amounts of petroleum available for use under defined circumstances.

Definitions

Proved reserves are those currently available for production and economical to produce at expected prices. Companies and governments determine proved reserves on the basis of drilling results, production experience and historical trends.

Probable reserves are additional amounts of economically recoverable crude oil or natural gas believed to exist on the basis of geological information.

Federal and provincial governments in Canada often cite figures for *established reserves*, which allow for anticipated crude oil and natural gas prices. Established reserves of natural gas are approximately equal to the sum of proved reserves plus one-half of probable reserves. Estimates of established reserves of crude oil are

more variable because they depend on assumptions about economics and technology such as enhanced oil recovery methods.

Recoverable resources include proved and probable reserves as well as those that can be produced with current technology but are not economical to produce at present.

Productive capacity, also known as producibility or available supply, is the estimated maximum daily volume that can be produced from proved reserves. This is based on reservoir characteristics, economic considerations, regulatory limitations and the feasibility of additional drilling or production facilities. Allowances are made for potential losses due to maintenance and operational problems at processing facilities.

Because higher prices encourage greater recovery and production, a number of estimates of potential recovery and production rates may be prepared, depending on anticipated future crude oil and natural gas prices.

CANADA'S ESTABLISHED RESERVES OF CONVENTIONAL CRUDE OIL
(millions of cubic metres)

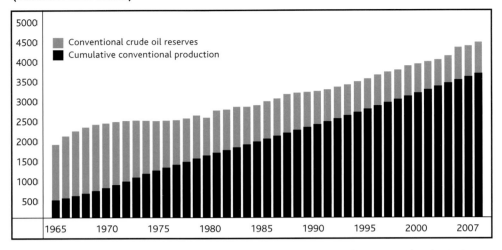

Source: Canadian Association of Petroleum Producers

CANADA'S ESTABLISHED RESERVES OF MARKETABLE NATURAL GAS
(billions of cubic metres)

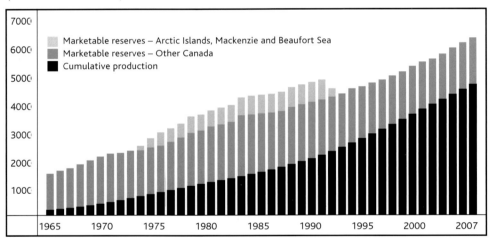

Source: Canadian Association of Petroleum Producers

Note: Remaining marketable natural gas reserves decline in 1992 and 1993 because the Canadian Association of Petroleum Producers discontinued the practice of carrying reserves for the Arctic Islands & Mackenzie Delta/Beaufort Sea respectively.

World proved reserves

Annual estimates compiled by the *Oil and Gas Journal* are used in many international comparisons of crude oil and natural gas reserves. Prior to 2003, the "unconventional" bitumen reserves in the Alberta oil sands were not included in the crude oil reserve figures. As of December 2002, the *Journal* decided to include 27.7 billion cubic metres of oil sands bitumen in Canada's total proved crude oil reserves of 28.4 billion cubic metres. Otherwise, the *Journal* continued to cite Canadian conventional crude oil and condensate reserves as reported by the Canadian Association of Petroleum Producers. The massive addition was based on the amount of bitumen that the Alberta Energy and Utilities Board (now Alberta Energy Resources Conservation Board) considers recoverable with existing technology. As a result, Canada now trails only Saudi Arabia in proved crude oil reserves in the world. Previously, Canada did not even rank in the top 20 countries with the most proved crude oil reserves. The new reserves estimate reflects the fact that oil sands bitumen now accounts for nearly 206,000 cubic metres per day of production and continues to increase. Some analysts, however, have questioned the new assessment.

CANADIAN ULTIMATE RECOVERABLE CONVENTIONAL CRUDE OIL RESERVES
(millions of cubic metres)

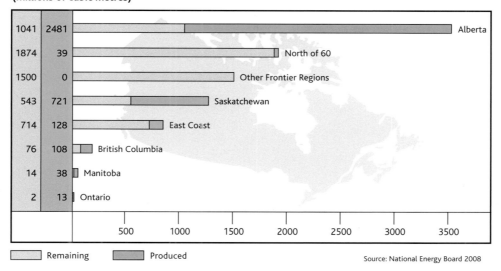

Remaining	Produced	Region
1041	2481	Alberta
1874	39	North of 60
1500	0	Other Frontier Regions
543	721	Saskatchewan
714	128	East Coast
76	108	British Columbia
14	38	Manitoba
2	13	Ontario

Remaining Produced

Source: National Energy Board 2008

CANADIAN ULTIMATE NATURAL GAS RESOURCE POTENTIAL
(billions of cubic metres)

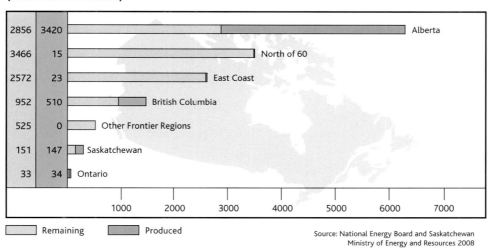

Remaining	Produced	Region
2856	3420	Alberta
3466	15	North of 60
2572	23	East Coast
952	510	British Columbia
525	0	Other Frontier Regions
151	147	Saskatchewan
33	34	Ontario

Remaining Produced

Source: National Energy Board and Saskatchewan
Ministry of Energy and Resources 2008

WORLD PROVED CRUDE OIL RESERVES
(billions of cubic metres, January 2009)

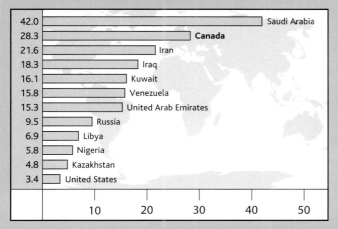

42.0	Saudi Arabia
28.3	**Canada**
21.6	Iran
18.3	Iraq
16.1	Kuwait
15.8	Venezuela
15.3	United Arab Emirates
9.5	Russia
6.9	Libya
5.8	Nigeria
4.8	Kazakhstan
3.4	United States

Source: *Oil and Gas Journal*

WORLD PROVED NATURAL GAS RESERVES
(trillions of cubic metres, January 2009)

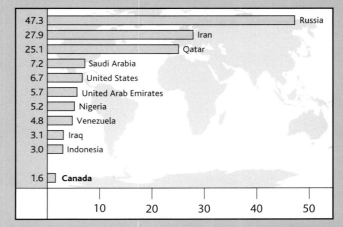

47.3	Russia
27.9	Iran
25.1	Qatar
7.2	Saudi Arabia
6.7	United States
5.7	United Arab Emirates
5.2	Nigeria
4.8	Venezuela
3.1	Iraq
3.0	Indonesia
1.6	**Canada**

Source: *Oil and Gas Journal*

Meeting people's needs

Canada has evolved into a relatively affluent society with a modern industrial economy adapted to our particular environment – vast land areas and coastal waters, northern climate, and great wealth in natural resources. Four-fifths of Canadians live in cities and suburbs, most located within a few hundred kilometres of the U.S. border. The close relationship with a neighbouring population and economy almost 10 times larger is a big factor in Canadian life and prosperity. The Canadian oil and gas industry is an integral part of this continental economy.

Reliable and affordable energy supplies have been crucial for economic development in Canada and worldwide. The income from energy exports has also contributed to Canada's current level of development. Crude oil and natural gas account for 75 per cent of Canada's primary energy supply, with the remainder coming from coal, hydroelectricity, nuclear plants, and renewable sources such as wood and wind. Beginning in 2001, energy exports overtook forest products for the first time as Canada's largest single category of foreign trade revenues. More than 90 per cent of our primary energy exports in 2007 were natural gas and crude oil; the other energy exports were coal (3.3 per cent) and electricity (3.7 per cent). Some of the electricity was generated from natural gas.

Energy and the economy

Compared to most countries, Canada seems to have done a good job of meeting the energy needs of the present generation. We produce more energy than we use. However, there are important questions that must be considered. How are we affecting the ability of future generations to meet their needs? What about the rest of the world?

Supplying energy is a never-ending task. For each cubic metre of crude oil and natural gas that is produced and consumed, another must be found somewhere. Wells typically produce most during the first year they are tapped, although some production may continue for decades. The easy-to-find resources have already been discovered. An increasing amount of Canadian petroleum will therefore come from remote and challenging environments such as the offshore and the Arctic, or from the application of technology to resources such as the Alberta oil sands and producing natural gas from coal There will also be stepped-up efforts to recover more of the hydrocarbons left underground by current and former production methods. Similar trends are occurring in all of the world's petroleum producing areas.

The International Energy Agency predicts world crude consumption will grow 25 per cent from 2008 to 2030, and the National Energy Board expects Canadian crude oil requirements to increase at least 45 per cent during the same period. The NEB also forecasts a 45 per cent increase from 2005 to 2030 in Canadian natural gas demand. Yet the additional reserves discovered – in Canada and worldwide – have barely kept pace with current production in recent years despite record levels of drilling activity. U.S. reserves of both crude oil and natural gas rose slightly during 2001 but have been on a downtrend for several decades. A notable exception is Canadian crude oil reserves, which were deemed to have increased since 1996 because more oil sands developments were announced.

Neither Canada nor the world will "run out" of crude oil and natural gas for a long time, but huge investments and a great deal of new technology will be needed to keep pace with the expected growth in consumption. There are political risks in some of the areas with the largest conventional crude oil reserves, such as the Middle East and the Caspian Sea region, and technology is continuing to evolve for non-conventional resources such as deepwater offshore crude oil and natural gas, Canadian oil sands bitumen and Venezuelan heavy oil. Much of the world's undeveloped natural gas is located far from consuming markets or in non-conventional sources such as methane trapped in coalbeds or methane hydrates (crystals of water and methane trapped on the ocean floors and in permafrost).

Some of the anticipated demand can be reduced by conservation – more efficient vehicles, greater use of public transit, and better-insulated buildings – and some can be met by alternative fuels such as methanol (wood alcohol), ethanol (grain alcohol), biodiesel (refined vegetable oil and rendered animal fat) or even hydrogen. The fastest-growing use for natural gas since the early 1990s has been to generate electricity. Some natural gas-fired electricity may be displaced in future by power from wind, solar, hydroelectric, geothermal, "clean coal" or nuclear technologies. However, everything points to continued growth in demand for Canadian crude oil and natural gas in the decades ahead. Meeting that demand will not be easy.

Photo courtesy of Brian Harder

Society and the environment

The intensified search for new energy supplies for the 21st century coincides with increased scientific knowledge about the effects of industrial activity on the environment. There is also a widespread consensus that the public and other stakeholders need to be consulted about decisions affecting them. Some related developments in Canada include:

- growing population in a number of key petroleum-producing areas
- competition among interests such as recreation, fishing, forestry and agriculture for use of publicly owned resources
- efforts to address the rights and needs of Aboriginal communities
- commitments to reduce greenhouse gas emissions and other environmental impacts, and
- increased development of renewable energy sources.

Every aspect of the petroleum industry – from exploration to the final use of its products – affects people, animals, plants, soil, air and water. Some effects are confined to a small area, while others have global implications. The effects of these activities, all of which are regulated by governments, must be balanced against the economic and social benefits the industry provides. The industry also contributes to scientific knowledge about the environment and encourages efficient use of energy. In some instances, crude oil and natural gas replace other energy sources such as coal that have greater environmental impacts.

Many environmental issues are difficult to resolve. In 1992, for example, Canada and other industrial countries signed the United Nations Framework Convention on Climate Change, a treaty pledging to stabilize emissions of greenhouse gases linked to global climate change – mainly carbon dioxide, methane and nitrogen oxides—"at a level that would prevent dangerous anthropogenic [human-induced] interference with the climate system." In fact, however, emissions continued to increase. The Canadian oil and gas industry reduced many of its own emissions, on a unit-of-production basis, but this was offset by increased production to meet domestic and export demand. According to Environment Canada, about one-sixth of Canada's total greenhouse gas emissions come from petroleum production, transportation and refining processes. However, the majority of petroleum-related emissions occur at the point of final use, such as a furnace or vehicle engine.

The oil and gas industry is making significant progress in addressing other social and environmental issues. Many initiatives are under way to reduce effects on local and regional air quality, water resources, land and biological diversity. There have been demonstrated successes such as the reduction in flaring and venting of natural gas in Western Canada (which also reduced greenhouse gas emissions) and the reduced exposure of workers and the public to toxic benzene emissions. Consultation with stakeholders is now an integral part of companies' planning and operations. Within the industry, information-sharing and environmental management systems help companies to keep pace with scientific knowledge and public expectations. Many companies subscribe to the goal of continuous improvement in social and environmental performance, recognizing that these ongoing commitments need to be improved constantly over time.

The challenge: global climate change

During the last few decades, the petroleum industry has made progress in improving energy efficiency. The amount of carbon compounds emitted to produce a given amount of gross domestic product (carbon intensity) has been reduced throughout the economy. However, rising population and economic growth have increased Canada's total emissions of greenhouse gases such as carbon dioxide. The oil and gas industry faces a major challenge in decreasing greenhouse gas emissions while also ensuring continued economic stability.

The greenhouse effect, which traps heat in the atmosphere, is a natural phenomenon that is essential to life on Earth. If there were no greenhouse effect, the Earth's average temperature would drop by about 33° C, to about -18° C. Most climate scientists believe that increased levels of carbon dioxide (CO_2) and other gases in the atmosphere produced by human activities are increasing the greenhouse effect. This could raise average global temperatures over time.

Causes of the greenhouse effect include water vapour (H_2O), carbon dioxide (CO_2), methane (CH_4) and nitrous oxide (N_2O). Water vapour is, in fact, the most prevalent factor in the greenhouse effect, but it has not been determined how or if human activities are affecting water vapour in the atmosphere. Among the gases produced by human activities, CO_2 has the biggest total effect because it is so much more abundant than the other gases. The warming caused by a tonne of methane, the main component of natural gas, is about 21 times greater than the warming from a tonne of CO_2. Methane is released into the atmosphere by agriculture and landfills as well as by oil and gas industry activities. Nitrous oxide, 310 times as potent as CO_2, is a by-product of fuel combustion in engines and furnaces. Other, even more potent greenhouse gases released by human activities include chlorofluorocarbons (CFCs), hydrofluorocarbons (HFCs), perfluorocarbons (PFCs), ozone (O_3) and sulphur hexafluoride (SF_6).

THE GREENHOUSE GAS EFFECT

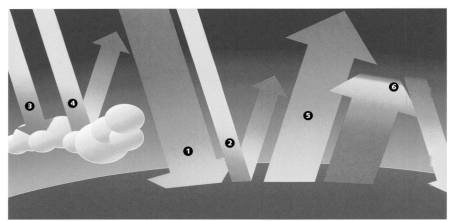

❶ Solar energy penetrates the Earth's surface

❷ A portion of the radiation is reflected off the Earth's surface

❸ Clouds absorb some radiation

❹ Clouds reflect part of the radiation

❺ Most of the energy absorbed by the Earth's surface is re-emitted as infrared radiation

❻ Greenhouse gases absorb and re-emit some of the radiation, heating the Earth's surface and lower atmosphere

Source: Environment Canada

Canada, with 0.5 per cent of the world's population, accounts for about 2.5 per cent of human-caused carbon dioxide emissions, 4.7 per cent of nitrous oxide and 5.1 per cent of methane emissions. This puts Canadians among the world's highest per-capita emitters of greenhouse gases. However, Canada has long, cold winters and occupies 6.5 per cent of the world's land area. Also, many Canadian industries are big energy users, and the nation is an exporter of crude oil, natural gas, coal, electricity, steel, aluminum and other energy-intensive products.

The Intergovernmental Panel on Climate Change (IPCC), a United Nations agency composed of hundreds of scientists from around the world, has been studying the effects of human-caused greenhouse gas emissions since 1988. In the IPCC's Fourth Assessment Report, issued in 2007, the scientists reached these conclusions:

- Warming of the climate system is unequivocal, as is now evident from observations of increases in global average air and ocean temperatures, widespread melting of snow and ice and rising global average sea level.
- Most of the observed increase in global average temperatures since the mid-20th century is *very likely* due to the observed increase in anthropogenic GHG

concentrations. It is *likely* that there has been significant anthropogenic warming over the past 50 years averaged over each continent (except Antarctica).

- Continued GHG emissions at or above current rates would cause further warming and induce many changes in the global climate system during the 21st century that would very likely be larger than those observed during the 20th century.

Some scientists disagree that climate change is occurring as a result of the increase in greenhouse gases in the atmosphere. They suggest alternative interpretations, including:

- The increase in global mean temperature is within the range of natural variations of the Earth's temperature, some of which are attributable to variations in solar radiation.
- The current warming trend is simply part of a larger pattern of naturally occurring temperature changes the Earth has experienced over the past million years.
- In more recent history, there have been fluctuations such as a warming period in the 1940s followed by a moderate cooling period in the mid-1970s and a pronounced warming period in the 1980s.

The world community has decided that the risks of climate change are too serious to ignore. Canadian governments and the oil

and gas industry have been pursuing means to reduce greenhouse gas emissions since the early 1990s. In December 2002, Canada ratified the Kyoto Accord, obliging the nation to reduce its greenhouse gas emissions to six per cent below 1990 levels by 2012. In February 2003, the federal government committed $1.7 billion towards a climate change action package. The strategy includes measures to encourage conservation in the residential sector and support for renewable energy, in particular wind and solar power, as well as alternative fuels such as ethanol and biodiesel, clean-coal technology, hydrogen fuel cells and initiatives that store carbon rather than release it into the atmosphere.

In April 2003, the Canadian Association of Petroleum Producers (CAPP) released the Calculating Greenhouse Gas Emissions guide, which provides CAPP members with a standardized approach to benchmarking and estimating greenhouse gas emissions.

CAPP and its members said they intend to work with federal, provincial and territorial governments on a plan that allows Canadians to continue to benefit from the production and export of crude oil and natural gas while promoting technological advances that lead to long-term solutions to climate change.

CANADIAN GREENHOUSE GAS EMISSIONS – ALL SECTORS
CO$_2$ emissions (million tonnes CO$_2$ equivalent)

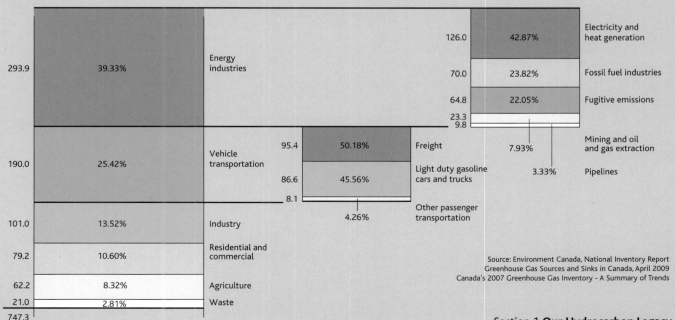

Source: Environment Canada, National Inventory Report
Greenhouse Gas Sources and Sinks in Canada, April 2009
Canada's 2007 Greenhouse Gas Inventory - A Summary of Trends

Safe workplaces

Training and equipment are crucial in maintaining safe workplaces in the oil and gas industry. Workers continually review safe practices, such as gripping the rails while descending a stairway, and emergency procedures such as boarding the rescue capsules on offshore platforms.

Photos courtesy of Alex MacAulay, Ocean Resources

Health and safety

The petroleum industry works closely with government authorities to protect the health and safety of workers and the public. Industry regulations reflect modern scientific knowledge about hazards and the technology available to reduce them.

Better technology, planning and training have led to a steady improvement in the industry's health and safety performance. New management systems designed to reward safe workplace behaviour have created operations that are not only safer for workers, but also for the public and the environment.

Examples of these health and safety initiatives include:

- sour gas drilling and production regulations, which along with specialized equipment and training, protect workers and the public from exposure to toxic concentrations of the hydrogen sulphide in sour gas
- improved vapour containment from production facilities to service stations reduces human exposure to volatile organic compounds, including potential cancer-causing compounds such as benzene; the refining industry has also reduced the benzene content of fuels
- automated equipment and remote control systems improve efficiency while reducing the potential for hazardous work situations in the industry, and
- sophisticated pipeline inspection devices, maintenance programs and monitoring systems reduce the number of pipeline accidents; pipelines are already the safest mode of commodity transportation in Canada.

The discussion in Section 2 includes more detail about the social, economic and environmental aspects of each component of the industry. Section 3, the conclusion, includes further discussion of the industry's role in sustainable development during the 21st century.

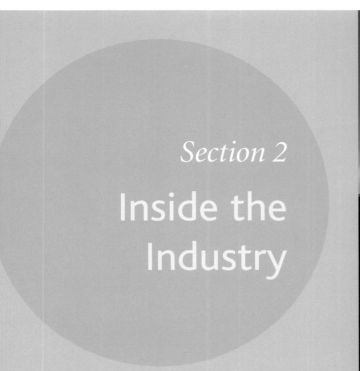

Section 2
Inside the Industry

An ever-expanding body of knowledge and continuing refinement of technologies and methods have combined to make the modern Canadian oil and gas industry efficient and effective in providing energy and products to consumers.

The amount of industry information stored and processed daily is staggering, and would have been unimaginable a few decades ago. Experts in companies, governments, research institutes and academic institutions analyze the information in search of better ways to find and produce crude oil and natural gas — at a lower cost, in greater volume, more safely and with fewer effects on the environment. There is a lot of co-operation, even between competitors. Certain information-sharing is required by government authorities in Canada, but the rest represents a voluntary effort to improve the performance of the industry as a whole.

New knowledge leads to the testing and deployment of new equipment and machinery, and new approaches to problems. In the oil sands, for example, more than $1 billion has been spent on research and development in the past two decades, with a further $25 million invested in collaborative research projects by universities and government in 2002. In 2005, six oil and gas companies with interests in the oil sands, spent $381 million on research and development, much of which was directed toward oil sands. According to the Oil Sands Developers Group (OSDG), formerly known as the Athabasca Regional Issues Working Group (RIWG), Alberta's oil sands

companies invest $75 to $100 million annually in research and development to improve both economic and environmental performance. As a result, the cost of producing a cubic metre of upgraded crude oil from bitumen has been halved since the 1970s, and emissions of sulphur dioxide have been reduced by about one-third since the early 1990s. These improvements were instrumental in the great expansion in oil sands production since the mid-1990s. Similar advances have occurred in every aspect of the industry.

This section examines each link in the chain connecting the initial search for petroleum to the point of final use.

Two features stand out in these discussions. The first is how far-reaching across Canada the industry is, extending in some way to every corner of a vast nation's geography.

The other distinguishing characteristic of the oil and gas industry is how much of it is invisible. The full scope of the industry is seldom evident. Not only is the resource itself buried, so are more than a half-million kilometres of pipelines and much of the storage for natural gas and natural gas liquids. Production and processing facilities are often in remote locations seldom seen by the general public.

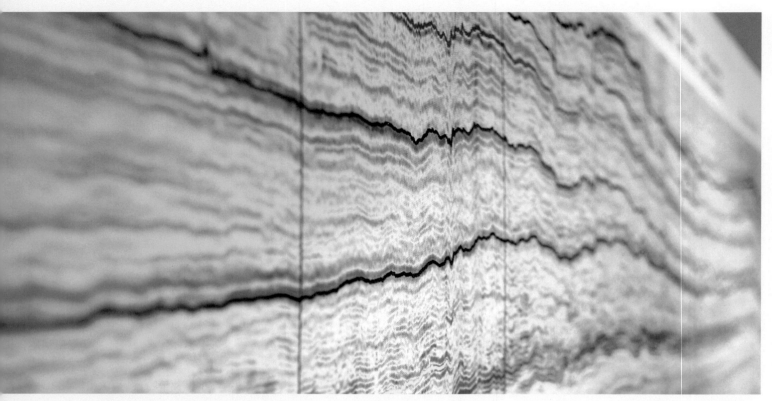

Photo courtesy of Brian Harder

The challenge

Where will we find the next cubic metre of crude oil or natural gas? Exploration provides the answers to that question. The challenge is to provide the most precise answers — quickly, efficiently, affordably, and with the fewest negative effects on people and the environment.

Exploration – the search for petroleum

The first, crucial component of the oil and gas industry is the search for new supplies to replace current production and meet future needs. The key steps in this process are locating the underground rock formations that may contain hydrocarbons, reaching agreements with the owners of surface and mineral rights in the area, and drilling wells to determine if the anticipated resources are actually there and can be produced economically.

Exploration in Canada builds on a century and a half of accumulated knowledge about the nation's geology – including some of the world's most comprehensive geological databases and sample collections. Advanced geophysical techniques, including low-impact seismic surveys and sophisticated computer programs, help to pinpoint the rock formations most likely to contain crude oil and natural gas. Companies and governments work closely with landowners, Aboriginals and other stakeholders in an effort to respect their rights and interests.

Anticlines in the Rockies

An anticline is one kind of rock formation that can "trap" hydrocarbons as they migrate towards the surface. This anticline is visible on a ridge in the Kananaskis range in Alberta.

Photo courtesy of Gord Hurlburt

Geology and geophysics

The petroleum industry provides employment for more than 500,000 people. This figure includes several thousand earth scientists or "explorationists" – mainly geologists and geophysicists – who guide the industry's search for oil and gas. The majority of their efforts have focused on the Western Canada Sedimentary Basin, the source of most current production, although they also study other current and potential petroleum-producing sedimentary basins in Canada and abroad.

Another key focus in recent years has been the East Coast offshore, where theories about the subsea geology are still evolving and there is a need for greater precision as large investments are considered in production facilities. Drilling a single well in the offshore can cost $20 million to $100 million or more, and production facilities can cost billions of dollars. Similar challenges await the oil and gas industry in the Arctic and off the West Coast. In the oil sands, the general characteristics of the resources are well

known – where the deposits are, how much bitumen they contain – but exploration techniques are still required to determine the exact locations and configurations for billion-dollar mining and steam-injection projects.

Looking inside rocks

Earth scientists in the petroleum industry, including specialists such as geochemists and paleontologists, study what has happened to rocks that may be buried thousands of metres below the surface, how those rocks were formed and affected by events stretching back millions of years, and how to identify traps where crude oil and natural gas may have accumulated within rock formations.

An explorationist may have a well-developed theory or intuition about why an area should contain crude oil and natural gas. A first-hand look at outcrop geology (rocks visible on the surface) and surface features sometimes helps to confirm the basic requirements – that there must be sedimentary rocks,

potential reservoir rock, potential traps and hydrocarbon-bearing source rocks in a sedimentary basin.

Within a basin, the explorer's first step is to examine all the information already known about the area. This might include academic papers, surface geology observations, records from previous wells drilled, data from agencies such as the Geological Survey of Canada or provincial government departments, and previous exploration results from nearby or similar areas. In Canada, government regulations ensure that much of the information obtained during exploration is recorded and eventually released publicly. This is often not the case in the United States and elsewhere around the world.

Geophysicists can identify the structure, configuration, thickness and depth of the rock layers within sedimentary basins by measuring slight variations in the Earth's gravitational and magnetic fields, and by measuring the time taken for seismic energy waves to

Common oil and gas traps

Traps are reservoir rock formations that halt the natural upward migration of hydrocarbons from the source rock to the surface. In a typical trap, gas accumulates on top of the reservoir as a "gas cap" over the "oil leg" which in turn overlies the water-saturated zone in the reservoir. This occurs because natural gas is lighter than oil, which is lighter than water. However, all three fluids are often intermingled in parts of the reservoir. Porosity is the ability of rock to hold oil and gas like water in a sponge. Permeability indicates how easily fluids can flow through the rock.

A trap requires three elements: a source for the oil and gas, typically black organic-rich shales; a porous reservoir rock, such as sandstone, limestone or dolomite, to accumulate the oil and gas; and an overlying impermeable rock to prevent the oil and gas from escaping.

Rock Types

 Surface gravels

Limestone

Sandstone

Shale

Salt

Reservoir Rocks

 Gas-bearing sandstone

 Oil-bearing sandstone

 Gas-bearing limestone

 Oil-bearing limestone

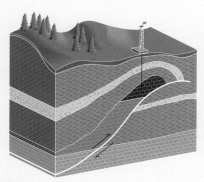

1 Thrust fault

In the foothills of Western Canada, east of the Rockies, the original limestone layer was first folded and then thrust-faulted over itself. An overlying seal of impermeable rock completes the structural trap. Examples include the Turner Valley oil and gas field and Jumping Pound gas field, both in southwestern Alberta.

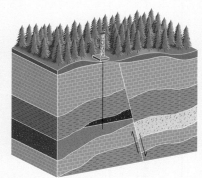

2 Normal fault

Faults drop one side down and push the other side up to place the reservoir rock against impermeable sealing rocks, forming a structural fault trap. An example is the Dunvegan gas field in northwestern Alberta.

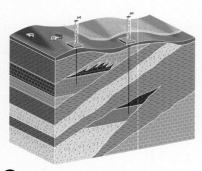

3 Stratigraphic pinch-out

This occurs where the porous limestone reservoir loses its porosity and becomes impermeable limestone, or the porous sandstone reservoir simply thins and pinches out. Overlying impermeable rocks act as seals. Examples include the D-1 Crossfield sour gas field and many oil and gas fields in Saskatchewan.

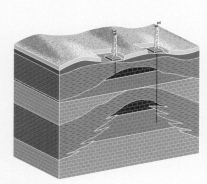

4 Reef

Porous ancient coral reefs grew in the warm seas that once covered much of Western Canada. They now provide prolific oil and gas reservoirs. Often overlying porous rock layers are "draped" or folded over the reefs and form separate traps. Overlying impermeable shales act as seals to the reservoirs. An example is the Leduc oil and gas field in Alberta.

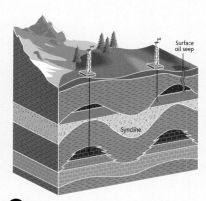

5 Anticlines

Where rock layers are folded into anticlines and synclines, the oil and gas migrate to the crests of the anticlines within the reservoir rock, and are trapped if overlain by an impermeable layer. If fractures occur, oil and gas may seep to the surface. Examples include the Bubbles and Jedney gas fields in northeastern British Columbia.

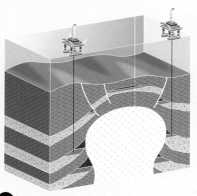

6 Salt dome

Under the weight of overlying rock layers, layers of salt will push their way toward the surface in salt domes and ridges. Oil and gas are trapped in folds and along faults above the dome and within upturned porous sandstones along the flanks of the dome. Examples are found off Canada's East Coast.

See also page 6: Cross section of the Western Canada Sedimentary Basin

©Canadian Centre for Energy Information 2009

pass through and be reflected from these sedimentary layers.

Fewer scientists, more science

Powerful computers have increased the productivity of scientists in the oil and gas industry. A single geologist or geophysicist, working at a personal computer, can now perform tasks that once required a large support staff of technologists, map makers, clerks and secretaries.

Increasingly, Canadians have been applying their skills and expertise to exploration problems elsewhere in the world. Some work for Canadian oil companies seeking to diversify abroad, and others are directly employed by foreign companies or provide services as consultants.

Industry experts are concerned, however, by the low number of young Canadians planning careers in earth sciences. In the late 1980s, the number of Canadian university graduates in geology and geophysics plummeted. Although enrollments have recovered somewhat since the mid-1990s, there is still concern about the number of earth scientists entering the industry.

Cuttings and cores

Results from previous drilling provide important information for explorationists. When a well is drilled, small rock chips called cuttings are ground up and broken off by the drill bit as it cuts into the rocks and is brought to the surface by drilling fluid. Geologists, geochemists and palynologists – scientists who study pollen and small fossils – examine the cuttings to learn more about the age, chemistry, porosity, permeability and other properties of the subsurface rock formations.

Larger, more continuous cylindrical rock samples, called cores, can also be cut using a special coring bit. Although coring adds to the cost of the well, laboratory analysis and visual examination of the core provide additional important details about the basin's history. Core analysis provides critical information on the composition and physical characteristics of the rock and any fluids within it.

Even if a well fails to encounter crude oil or natural gas in commercial quantities, it still provides valuable information about underground rocks and structures. This may allow explorationists to generate new prospects or to match up certain seismic patterns with corresponding rock formations, which can lead to success with the next well – or the one after that.

A comprehensive database

There has been long-standing and close co-operation among industry, government and scientists in gathering data about crude oil and natural gas in Canada. Early requirements to record accurately all kinds of information from the hundreds of thousands of wells drilled to date in Canada have given us an extremely valuable and reliable database that can be used quickly and cheaply.

The recent introduction of computerized commercial databases is speeding up the generation of new drilling prospects, the optimization of producing fields, and the evaluation of field operations.

In offshore areas, there are fewer clues available for targeting exploration, but some initial information can be obtained from detailed mapping of the ocean floor, samples of the seabed composition, and comparisons with the geology of nearby land areas and similar features elsewhere in the world.

Based on such observations, the explorationist must then convince managers or investors to provide funds for further work. The next stage is to develop an image of the underground formations integrating all the available geological and geophysical information. It may be possible to obtain the geophysical data from regulatory bodies or purchase information acquired in recent surveys. If not, the geologist works with a geophysicist and a contractor to plan a seismic survey. Obtaining a government licence and arranging access with landowners is next on the agenda. An environmental assessment is also required for all offshore exploration activities.

Core Samples
Cores are stored in government laboratories and made available to industry. They provide vital information for petroleum exploration.

©Canadian Centre for Energy Information 2009

Land – the basis of all wealth

Access to land, and the minerals beneath it, is the basis for all wealth in the upstream petroleum industry. Oil company land departments negotiate access with owners, make arrangements with joint venture partners and acquire crude oil and natural gas rights. Specialized land agents, traditionally known as landmen although they may be male or female, are responsible for all these negotiations.

Exploration companies deal with two types of real estate. Surface rights are the rights to work on the surface of the land. Mineral rights are the rights to explore for and produce the resources below the surface. The two kinds of rights are usually owned separately. Mineral rights may be owned by individuals called freeholders, who are usually the descendants of early settlers, by the federal government, or most commonly by a provincial government. Government-owned rights are referred to as Crown rights. Certain companies that own land "in fee" own both surface and mineral rights under land concessions granted by the federal government in the 19th century. The claim to Aboriginal ownership of substantial areas of both surface and mineral rights is being increasingly recognized across Canada.

In East Coast offshore areas, the federal and provincial governments own both the "surface" (water and seabed) and the mineral rights.

An economic calculation

Before deciding whether to invest in an exploration program, companies try to determine whether the well is likely to produce crude oil or natural gas, based on the geological and geophysical information that they have collected. They then make an economic calculation based on a number of factors:

- estimate of the geological risk
- amount of expected crude oil or natural gas production from a successful well
- likely selling price of the resource
- drilling and operating costs
- distance to processing facilities and pipelines
- taxes and royalties
- inflation and interest rates, and
- financial returns that might be earned by investing elsewhere.

The result tells companies if a geological prospect is worth exploring and how much they can afford to spend to acquire the mineral rights for a parcel of land. This can be a fairly precise calculation in established producing areas such as Western Canada. In newer exploration areas, such as the offshore, factors such as geological risk are more difficult to determine because fewer wells have been drilled.

Companies may decide the numbers are too discouraging and shelve the prospect until there is some change in economic conditions or an improvement in the geological knowledge of the area. They may decide to reduce the risk by asking the company's land department to find a partner.

Negotiations and onshore Crown land sales

In Canada's sedimentary basins, provincial and federal governments own the mineral rights under most of the land. If mineral rights are freehold, company land agents negotiate directly with the owner to acquire a "petroleum (crude oil) and natural gas lease." If the rights are already held or leased by another company, the agents will still have to acquire the rights by negotiating an agreement with the rights owner. Often the company will undertake exploration, usually by drilling a well, in exchange for an interest in the mineral rights and production. This type of agreement is known as a farmout. If the Crown mineral rights are not currently leased, the company must apply to the appropriate government agency to have the rights listed or posted for competitive bidding at a land sale.

Based on its economic calculations, the company submits a bid to the government or other mineral rights owner. Rights are then auctioned by posting the property's availability and asking for confidential bids from interested parties. The company with the highest bid obtains an exploratory permit, licence or lease. The amount paid at auctions for Crown mineral rights is known as a bonus payment. Whether freehold or Crown, the owner of mineral rights also receives a royalty, which is a share of any future production or equivalent revenue.

The terms of permits, licences or leases generally require that the holder begin exploration activity within a specified period. If a company cannot afford the work or wants to reduce the risk, its agents may farm out the land to others who can earn a share of production by undertaking exploration. At the end of the initial term of the lease, if the land has been drilled and crude oil or natural gas found, then the rights are held down to the deepest formation proved to be capable of production. The rights below that formation are returned to the Crown to be posted for future Crown land sales. This is referred to as "deep rights reversion."

Offshore and Arctic licences

Off the East Coast and in the Arctic, federal licences are auctioned to companies on the basis of spending commitments that must be honoured within a fixed period of time. If commercial quantities of crude oil or natural gas are found, the company retains the mineral rights. Initially, royalties are paid to the government at a low rate until exploration and development costs are recovered, at which time royalty rates escalate according to a set schedule. Under agreements with the federal government, the provinces of Nova Scotia and Newfoundland and Labrador establish the royalty rates for their offshore crude oil and natural gas and collect the royalties on production. Some Arctic regions have Aboriginal ownership as well as federal, and First Nations and Inuit entities issue their own permits or licences to conduct operations on their lands, subject to their own royalty regimes.

Surface rights

In addition to mineral rights and joint ventures, land departments must arrange surface access agreements for seismic surveys, wellsites, access roads and pipelines with the parties directly affected by exploration activities. These may include: landowners, other oil and gas companies, government departments, grazing lease holders and forestry companies. In areas where there are Aboriginal interests such as land claims, settlements or reserves, the communities are consulted regarding impacts of the proposed oil and gas activity on Aboriginal rights. In some regions, Aboriginal communities own the surface rights and negotiate agreements for access to the mineral rights.

Strict laws apply to an oil and gas company's use of surface rights. The company must lease the land from the surface owner, establish an annual rental fee for use of the land, and agree to pay for all damages or inconvenience caused by the presence of equipment or facilities. After operations cease, the company must reclaim agricultural land to "equivalent land capability" as regulated by most Canadian jurisdictions. If surface access cannot be negotiated for Crown mineral rights, right-of-entry may be obtained through a process known as "surface rights arbitration" whereby a quasi-judicial board can grant right-of-entry and rule on matters of compensation.

Companies try to locate wells, roads and pipelines where they will have the least impact on nearby residents and the environment. Topsoil is removed and stockpiled for use in eventual reclamation. The cleared area around the well, sometimes referred to as the "lease," is fenced off both to protect facilities and to avoid harm to human or animal trespassers.

Careers in energy

Careers in exploration and production include coring operators, directional drillers, environmental technologists, exploration geologists, geological and geophysical technologists, geophysicists, land agents, machinists, oceanographers, petroleum engineers and technologists, rig managers, seismic shooters, technical sales representatives, truck drivers and more.

Learn more about careers in energy at **www.centreforenergy.com**

In the offshore and the northern territories, regulatory boards require environmental assessments – including the potential impacts on fisheries and marine life – before all exploration and development activities begin.

Public involvement and stakeholders

Activities of the oil and gas industry often affect surrounding areas and populations. People with an interest in these activities are called stakeholders. They may include nearby residents, farmers and communities, Aboriginals, recreational land users, foresters, miners, fishing and shipping interests, local businesses, environmental groups and various government agencies as well as the operating company, its employees and contractors. Industry associations, government regulators and individual companies have policies and guidelines to make sure stakeholders are consulted about industry operations.

Depending on the operation and its impacts, the public consultation can take many different forms. Major projects may involve formal public hearings, while a small development may just be discussed informally with those directly affected. The methods used for consultation by the oil and gas industry include: public meetings, open houses, advisory committees, facility tours, meetings with town councils and community organizations, small group meetings, one-on-one meetings, workshop sessions, trade shows, telephone contacts, questionnaires, surveys, brochures, newsletters, exhibits, news releases, media interviews, advertisements and toll-free telephone numbers.

The consultation methods developed in Alberta, including a framework for alternative dispute resolution, have attracted attention across Canada and around the world. The Alberta system now serves as a model for other jurisdictions. Additional recent initiatives to improve consultation include community advisory groups established by communities and companies in Western Canada and the formation in Atlantic Canada of the Nova Scotia Petroleum-Fisheries Liaison Group and a similar group, One Ocean, between the fisheries and petroleum industries in Newfoundland and Labrador.

Protecting the marine environment

The Canada-Newfoundland Offshore Petroleum Board and the Canada-Nova Scotia Offshore Petroleum Board regulate all exploration, development and production operations to avoid impacts on fisheries, marine life, water quality and navigation. The National Energy Board and the federal Department of Fisheries and Oceans also regulate offshore oil and gas activities. Licences include requirements to seal off wells and remove subsea equipment when operations cease. Environmental impact assessments are required for all activities, and public hearings are conducted before approval of major projects. Research has identified marine species and sites that might be affected by offshore exploration and development, and one marine area off Nova Scotia, the Sable Gully, has been designated a marine protected area.

Typical land dispositions in Western Canada

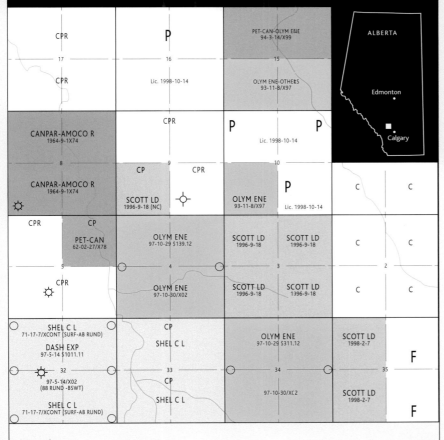

Petroleum landmen acquiring petroleum and natural gas rights rely heavily on specialized mineral ownership maps. These maps identify current mineral ownership, lands posted for sales, when rights expire and the amount paid for mineral rights. The petroleum and natural gas rights map shown below depicts an area measuring approximately four square miles located about 25 kilometres northwest of Calgary, Alberta. Because the land was surveyed prior to 1979, the grid is measured in miles rather than kilometres.

Legend

C	Crown land
F	Freehold lands undisposed
CPR	Canadian Pacific Railway lands (all oil and natural gas rights)
CP	Canadian Pacific Railway lands (oil rights only)
P	Crown lands posted for a land sale
OLYM ENE	Olympic Energy: (company that holds the lease); **$311.12** (bonus) paid per hectare
97-10-30/X02	Date acquired and the year that the lease expires (X02 = the year 2002)
35	Section number; each section is one mile square and contains 256 hectares
☼	Gas well
⋄	Dry and abandoned well
○	Depicts a Crown oil and gas lease

Source: Petroleum Information/Dwights

Land and biological diversity

Upstream oil and gas activities can affect plants and wildlife in several ways. The direct impacts occur when operations disrupt the habitat of a species – for example, by clearing land for well sites or seismic surveys. Indirect impacts result when the industry's roads and seismic cutlines create access for other users who disrupt the habitat. Linear developments such as roads, cutlines and pipeline rights-of-way can also affect wildlife by creating travel corridors for predators such as wolves. The industry works with stakeholders to reduce both kinds of effects on an area's biological diversity.

Biological diversity (also known as biodiversity) is the distribution and abundance of living organisms and the ecological systems of which they are a part. Biodiversity includes diversity within and between species and the diversity of ecosystems across a landscape. Recently, there has been an increasing focus on the "cumulative effects" of multiple activities in an area – such as forestry, mining, recreation, hunting and trapping, in addition to the oil and gas industry.

The first priority is to identify the species and habitats needing protection. Industry associations and companies work with scientists, government officials, landowners and interest groups to accomplish this. In Alberta, for example, the Special Places 2000 program identified and protected many environmentally sensitive areas. Companies have given up mineral rights in substantial areas of Western Canada, such as the Whaleback area in the Alberta foothills, to allow for creation of protected areas. The industry also funds and supports research on species such as woodland caribou and grizzly bears to determine how they are affected by operations. The federal Species at Risk Act provides additional protection for threatened and endangered species across Canada.

Wetlands conservation area in northern Alberta

Photo courtesy of Suncor Energy

Better methods of road design and site selection also reduce impacts on biodiversity. Gates may be used to control access into sensitive areas. Roads may be re-contoured and blocked with logs and rocks after operations cease, and bridges may be removed. Winter roads built on packed snow are used in some areas. Operations may be halted during wildlife breeding or migration seasons.

In some areas such as northeastern British Columbia and northern Alberta, drilling traditionally occurred during the winter when the soil was frozen. However, the use of wooden mats to protect the soil under roads and well sites has recently permitted drilling during warmer months as well. Mat technology gives companies more flexibility in planning drilling activities and reduces the "boom-and-bust" effect when all activity occurs in a short period.

Most land use by the oil and gas industry is temporary. Seismic crews conduct their surveys and move on.

The average well produces for about 20 to 25 years. Other facilities will be shut down as resources are depleted and new technologies emerge. Today, the plans for all operations and facilities include provisions for the eventual reclamation of the sites. Wherever possible, sites are restored to equivalent land capability. Operating companies continue to be responsible for sites until reclamation is complete.

Directional and horizontal drilling technologies allow companies to locate operations where they will have the least impact on plants and wildlife. It is now possible to drill many wells from a single site. This reduces the number of roads, power lines and pipelines needed to serve the site, and the amount of land that eventually needs to be reclaimed. Hydrotransport, a new method of moving mined oil sand by pipeline instead of conveyor belts, reduces land disturbance by oil sands projects.

The oil and gas industry has joined with the forest industry to develop a new approach to road and site planning called integrated landscape management. The goal is to reduce the cumulative effects from multiple users of the landscape.

When sites are reclaimed, they may be replanted with native plant species rather than commercial seed mixes. Research is under way to improve the success of native species on reclaimed land and to increase the variety of species used in reclamation.

For decommissioning industrial sites such as natural gas processing plants and oil processing facilities, companies work out detailed, long-term plans in consultation with regulators and other stakeholders such as landowners, municipalities and Aboriginal communities.

©Canadian Centre for Energy Information 2009

Seismic surveys

Geophysicists use seismic surveys to develop "pictures" of underground rock formations. The surveys are based on how different rock types reflect energy waves back to the surface. The technique is similar to the way that sonar helps to map the sea bottom or ultrasound looks inside the human body.

Onshore surveys

In an onshore seismic survey, the geophysical contractor's crew lays out a line or several lines of sensitive receivers, called geophones or "jugs," on the ground. Explosions or mechanical vibrations are then created at "shot points" on the surface, and the geophones record the energy reflected back as seismic waves from rock layers at various depths. Cables usually connect the geophones and the recording instruments, but recently wireless telemetry has sometimes been used to relay the information with radio waves. The crew then moves to the next set of shot points to repeat the process.

Detonation of dynamite charges in shallow holes has been the traditional method of generating energy waves for onshore seismic surveys. To reduce environmental impact, many contractors today use the mechanical vibroseis method to send energy waves from a heavy, vibrating vehicle into the ground. (see illustration, page 46)

In sensitive areas of Western Canada and the North, the use of low-impact and helicopter-portable seismic equipment has reduced the environmental effects of seismic surveys. Seismic crews use cutlines as narrow as 1.5 metres, just enough for line-of-sight surveying, instead of the previous practice of clearing a five-metre route for wheeled or tracked equipment. The narrow cutlines grow back quickly, minimizing both the direct and indirect impacts. Recent seismic developments include positioning shot points from helicopters and using global positioning systems, thus eliminating the need for cutlines entirely. In certain instances, companies work with local conservation groups and forestry companies to plan seismic surveys to make maximum use of existing trails and avoid sites such as bird nesting areas. Packhorses have been used to carry equipment in some mountainous and forested areas.

Offshore surveys

In offshore exploration, "air guns" using compressed air have replaced dynamite as a better, safer energy source that also minimizes the impact on marine life. A marine vessel records the reflected energy from a towed array of hydrophones, similar to the geophones used on land. In shallow waters, the hydrophones may be laid out on the seabed. (see illustration, page 47)

In the offshore, seismic activities are restricted during fish spawning seasons and when sensitive species might be affected. In areas frequented by fish and marine mammals, the sound level is increased gradually at the beginning of a survey so that the fish and mammals have an opportunity to move out of the area.

Data processing

Geophysicists use powerful computers and specialized software to process the data from digitally recorded seismic surveys. The computers filter extraneous "noise" and enhance the desired signals to identify different rock layers and structures. This is accomplished by calculating the intensity and wave patterns of the reflected sound waves and the time it takes for them to travel through the rocks and back to the surface.

Two dimensions and more

The data from a single line of geophones gives a two-dimensional or 2D view, like a single slice through an apple. A newer type of seismic survey, processing of the data from several lines of geophones, creates a three-dimensional or 3D image of the geology below, and may show the location and extent of porous layers within these structures. In an apple, a 3D survey might show the dimensions of a worm hole missed entirely in the 2D picture. While 3D is considerably more expensive, it can provide vital information about the extent of a formation identified initially by 2D techniques or by previous exploration in an area.

A new technique called four-dimensional or 4D seismic involves shooting 3D seismic repeatedly in the same location, at intervals months or years apart, to observe changes as crude oil or natural gas is drawn out of the reservoir, and to identify areas where oil or gas remains. In the apple analogy, it would be like watching the worm's progress over time.

Seismic surveys are most useful where the rocks consist of layers of different thickness and hardness or where the rocks are folded or faulted into possible crude oil and natural gas traps. Geophysicists and geologists examine the seismic data for the presence of suitable traps and for similarities with other petroleum-producing areas. If the results seem promising, they use the seismic data to pinpoint where and how deep to drill a well.

Seismic surveys are particularly important in offshore areas, where precise information is needed before investing tens of millions of dollars in exploratory wells. From 1960 to 2001, a total of 377,299 kilometres of 2D seismic was shot off Nova Scotia, and from 1985 to 2001, 3D surveys were conducted over an area of 23,944 square kilometres. Off Newfoundland and Labrador, 158,584 kilometres of seismic were shot during 2001 alone. A new seismic survey was also shot in the Beaufort Sea in 2002.

No matter how much is known about the geology and geophysics of an area, the only way to know for certain if rocks contain commercial quantities of crude oil or natural gas is to drill a well. The next section describes how this is done.

Testing a theory

An example of evolving geological knowledge is the current theory about the Atlantic margin. This view maintains that rich deposits of hydrocarbons should be found at the bottom of the sloping edge of the continental shelf off Nova Scotia. Seismic surveys seemed to confirm the geologists' theories, but only recently has there been the combination of drilling technology, investment capital and market demand to justify drilling wells in waters more than a kilometre deep. In 2002, the Annapolis G-24 well 345 kilometres south of Halifax struck natural gas at a total well depth of 6,100 metres from the platform to the bottom of the well; the water depth at the location was 1,675 metres.

Vibroseis 3D seismic method

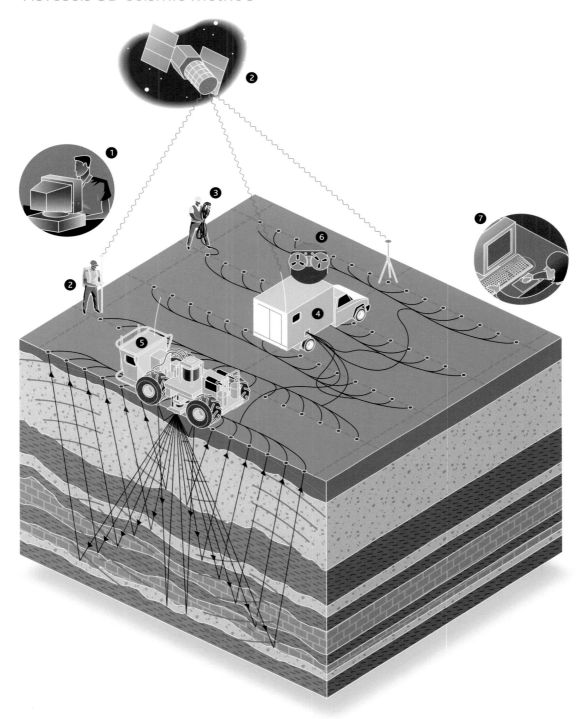

1. Company plans and designs a seismic program.

2. Surveyors use satellite-based global positioning system (GPS) to precisely position source and receiver locations.

3. Seismic crew members lay out cables and geophones.

4. Cables are attached to recording system.

5. Vibrator trucks generate a controlled vibration force of up to 32,000 kilograms at each source point.

6. Underlying geologic structures reflect some of the vibrations back to the surface where the geophones convert them into electrical impulses that are recorded on magnetic tape.

7. Magnetic tapes are sent for processing and interpretation of the recorded data.

©Canadian Centre for Energy Information 2009

Marine seismic survey

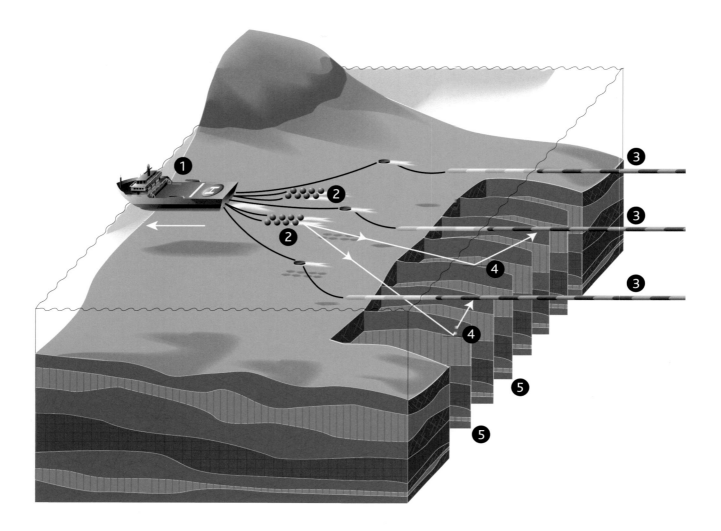

Steps involved in a marine seismic survey

Company plans and designs seismic program.

1 Ship navigates along a series of straight lines above the survey area

2 Ship tows energy sources, usually arrays of airguns, to produce sound energy in the water

3 Ship also tows long "streamers," between three and six kilometres in length, filled with hundreds of underwater microphones called hydrophones.

As the ship moves slowly along each survey line, a series of controlled bursts of compressed air from the airguns in the water generate sufficient energy to travel deep into the earth below the ocean floor.

4 When this energy is reflected back from underlying geologic strata, it is detected by the hydrophones that convert the energy into electrical impulses which are then transmitted back along the streamers to the ship to be recorded on magnetic tape.

The data on the magnetic tapes are processed, often onboard the vessel, to create images of the subsurface.

5 The result is a series of lines of recorded seismic data that together yield a graphic 3D representation of subsurface geologic structure, enabling interpreters to decide where to drill for oil or gas.

©Veritas DGC Inc./Canadian Centre for Energy Information 2009

Photo courtesy of Shell Canada

The challenge

Drillers aim to complete wells safely, quickly and cost-effectively, with minimum disturbance of the environment. The primary objective is a commercial quantity of crude oil or natural gas, but even a "dry hole" can provide valuable information about an area's geology.

Drilling – the moment of truth

Drillers turn theory into hard economic reality. Even when a well is located right between two producing wells, there is still a risk that nothing will be found – and also the possibility of greater-than-expected success. The stakes are much higher when the well is a "wildcat," the term for a well in previously unexplored territory.

In addition to financial risks, drillers must deal with other issues including environmental impacts on land, water and air; safety of workers and nearby residents; unexpected equipment failures and reservoir problems; remote locations, and weather extremes. About one-third of the natural gas in Western Canada is "sour" – containing toxic hydrogen sulphide – and this poses additional challenges for drillers. Extra precautions are taken to prevent releases of sour gas that might endanger workers or nearby populations.

Producers, contractors and government officials work together to reduce the risks. They do this through planning, training, equipment selection, standards and regulated procedures. Canadians are world leaders in some specialties such as sour gas drilling, horizontal and multi-lateral drilling, environmental protection, on-ice drilling and cold weather operations.

Top-drive drilling

Photo courtesy of Tesco Corporation

Drilling was the most severely affected activity in the industry slowdown from 1986 to 1992, and it enjoyed the strongest growth as activity recovered in the mid-1990s. Drilling activity set all-time records in 1997, 2000, 2001, 2003, 2004 and 2005. During that time, the number of wells drilled increased almost 50 per cent to 26,951 from 18,104. From 2005 to 2007, the number of wells drilled decreased 21 per cent to 21,210. More than two-thirds of the wells drilled since 1997 have targeted natural gas.

In 2003, the Canadian service industries sector – composed of drilling contractors, service and supply companies and geophysical services – employed some 95,000 workers. The drilling sector includes direct employees of drilling and service rig contractors, and other oil workers in oil field service and supply companies.

Sophisticated drilling techniques

During the exploration and drilling slowdown from 1986 to 1992, many experienced drillers and rig hands left the industry or took their skills abroad. Increased activity in Canada since the mid-1990s meant that new workers had to be trained to operate the sophisticated rigs and associated drilling equipment. Drilling operations have become more complex to satisfy government regulations and customer demands, and to find new reservoirs in intensively developed producing areas.

Advances in the last decade include:
- new types of drilling rigs using top drives and coiled tubing
- new ways of drilling such as horizontal and multi-lateral wells, underbalanced drilling and drilling with casing

- sophisticated new technology such as downhole surveying and downhole motors
- better drilling bits
- improved methods of transmitting information and commands to and from downhole equipment
- environmentally acceptable drilling fluids and mud systems, and
- improved logging equipment to assess well conditions far below ground.

Breakthroughs have occurred in all areas, and the use of computers to monitor, record and analyze information helps make it possible to drill wells more quickly, economically and safely. These advances have been evident in both onshore and offshore drilling.

Methods of drilling

Until the 1930s, most wells in Canada were drilled with cable-tool drilling rigs. A heavy bit, suspended from a cable, was dropped repeatedly to carve out a hole. This simple, inexpensive method is still used occasionally in historic Ontario oilfields and for other purposes such as drilling water wells.

By far the most common drilling method in Canada today is rotary drilling. The bit is attached to the bottom of a rotating pipe. Traditionally the pipe was turned by a rotating table on the rig floor, but an increasing number of rigs today use top drives – electric or hydraulic motors that move up and down in the drill rig at the top of the drill pipe.

In addition, many drilling activities today are performed with downhole motors that turn the bit. The motor and bit are attached to the end of a long tube that does not rotate. The circulation of drilling fluid (mud) transmits energy to the bit by means of a downhole motor. Downhole motors are also used in combination with rotary drilling rigs to drill directional and horizontal holes.

Truck-mounted service rigs are used for maintenance on existing wells. They are used mainly for raising and lowering equipment and instruments, and do not perform actual drilling.

Drilling contractors

Rig utilization rates fluctuate year by year, influenced by such things as commodity prices, weather, and crew availability. Since 2000, rig utilization has varied from a low of 43 per cent in 2007 to a high of 71.2 per cent in 2005. In 2008, an average of 405 rotary drilling rigs were operating in Canada out of a total fleet of 863 rigs for an average utilization rate of 46.9 per cent. Most rigs are owned by contractors who market their services to exploration and production companies. A few producers operate their own rigs. The cost of a well can range from $50,000 for a shallow land-based well to $10 million or more for a deep well in Western Canada and up to $80 million or more for one in deep water offshore. Arctic onshore wells are at least 25 per cent more expensive than comparable wells in Western Canada, mainly due to higher transportation costs

for the rig, supplies and workers, and some onshore Arctic wells cost up to $30 million.

There are many different types of rigs, commonly known as singles, doubles or triples based on how many 9.5-metre lengths of pipe can be connected together and stacked in the derrick. As a general rule, the bigger the rig, the deeper it can drill. The smallest are mounted on trucks, while the largest are installed on ships or offshore platforms. Some are specially equipped for sour gas exploration, Arctic operations, slanted holes or horizontal drilling.

Land-based rigs can be quickly assembled and taken apart in sections for moving between locations, although this may require up to 60 semi-trailers. Another 50 loads are required to transport the necessary cement, drilling fluids, casing, fuel tanks and testing equipment. Companies decide which kind of rig to use on a given well on the basis of cost, availability, depth, site and reservoir characteristics, and the type of well to be drilled. Sour gas drilling rigs, for example, include special safety equipment. Rigs for

drilling in the Northwest Territories have additional insulation. Some rigs can be slanted to drill directional wells.

Before the rig arrives on a site, contractors will have already built the access road and prepared the pad on which the rig is installed. Plastic, clay and earth are used to create barriers so that any spills can be contained. The rig itself is hinged so that it unfolds like a jackknife as cables and sheaves (pulleys) hoist it into the upright position. The other components – such as the motor controls, blowout preventers, pumps and mud mixing equipment – are all designed in modules for easy hookup. The assembly process is known as "rigging up."

Elsewhere in the world, helicopter-portable drilling rigs have been used in remote areas such as Indonesian jungles. Such rigs have not been used in Canada to date because roads are generally needed to meet safety regulations – which require an evacuation route for workers in case of an emergency during which flying might not be possible. Road transportation is also more economical for delivering supplies and moving the rig.

CANADIAN DRILLING ACTIVITY TOTALS
(number of wells drilled)

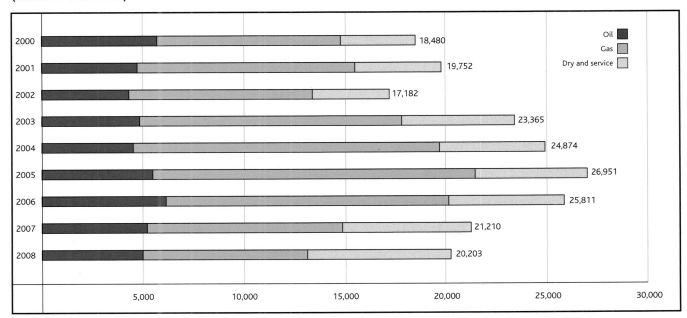

Year	Total
2000	18,480
2001	19,752
2002	17,182
2003	23,365
2004	24,874
2005	26,951
2006	25,811
2007	21,210
2008	20,203

Oil / Gas / Dry and service

* Includes suspended wells and many natural gas from coal (coalbed methane) wells not yet in production.

Source: Canadian Association of Petroleum Producers

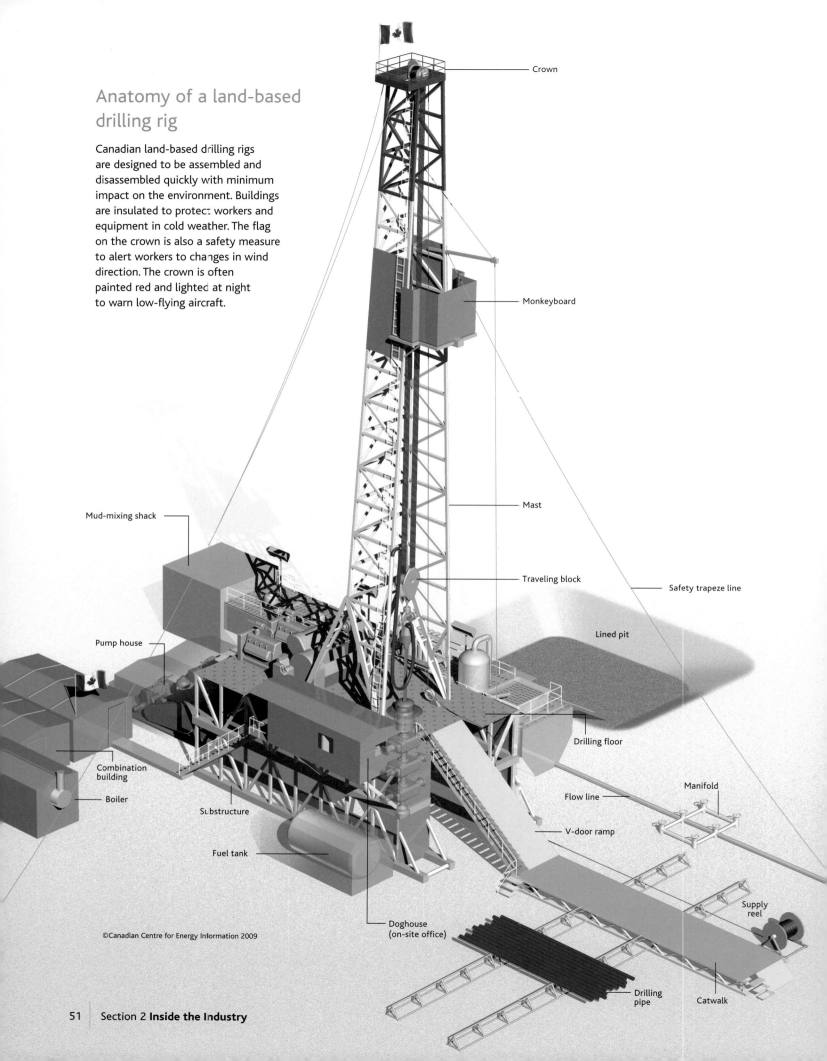

Anatomy of a land-based drilling rig

Canadian land-based drilling rigs are designed to be assembled and disassembled quickly with minimum impact on the environment. Buildings are insulated to protect workers and equipment in cold weather. The flag on the crown is also a safety measure to alert workers to changes in wind direction. The crown is often painted red and lighted at night to warn low-flying aircraft.

Crown

Monkeyboard

Mast

Traveling block

Safety trapeze line

Lined pit

Mud-mixing shack

Pump house

Combination building

Boiler

Substructure

Fuel tank

Drilling floor

Doghouse (on-site office)

Flow line

Manifold

V-door ramp

Supply reel

Drilling pipe

Catwalk

©Canadian Centre for Energy Information 2009

Rotating systems

CONVENTIONAL DRILLING

On most land-based rigs, a rotary table on the rig floor rotates the kelly, which turns the drill pipe and drill bit. As the drill bit penetrates deeper, the crew threads additional pipe onto the top of the drill string. Sections of pipe are typically 9.5 metres long, but may be longer; diameters and wall thickness also vary, depending on well depth.

TOP DRIVE DRILLING

Top drive drilling replaces the kelly method of rotation used in conventional rotary drilling. A hydraulic or electric motor is suspended above the drill pipe and enables the top drive rig to rotate and pump continuously while drilling or during the removal of drill pipe from the hole. Most offshore units and an increasing number of land rigs use top drives.

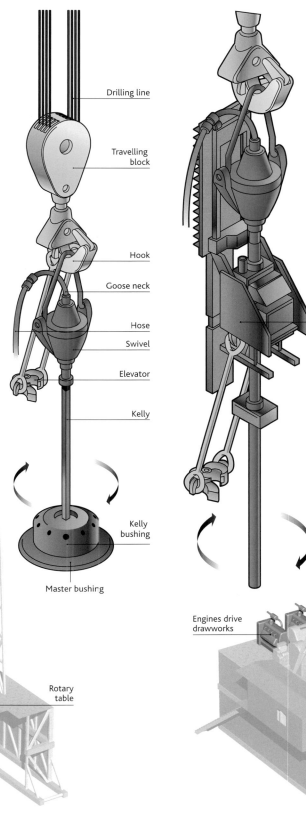

Drilling line

Travelling block

Hook

Goose neck

Hose

Swivel

Elevator

Kelly

Kelly bushing

Master bushing

Hydraulic motor

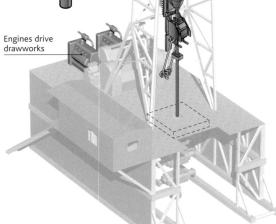

Engines drive the drawworks and the rotary table, which rotates the kelly

Rotary table

Engines drive drawworks

©Canadian Centre for Energy Information 2009

Mud motor

One technique used in horizontal drilling employs a mud motor that turns the bit. The motor, a downhole hydraulic drive, is placed behind the bit at the bottom of the length of drill pipe and receives power from the mud flow to turn the bit. The slotted liners in this illustration are inserted after the completion of drilling to facilitate the flow of oil into the well.

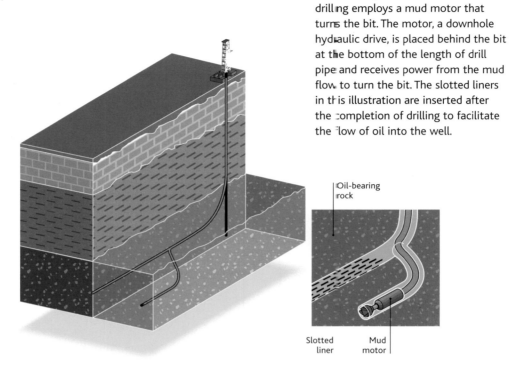

Oil-bearing rock

Slotted liner

Mud motor

©Canadian Centre for Energy Information 2009

Hoisting system

The hoisting system works as an elaborate pulley to lift the traveling block and remove the drill pipe. This action enables the installation of an extra length of pipe or a new drill bit.

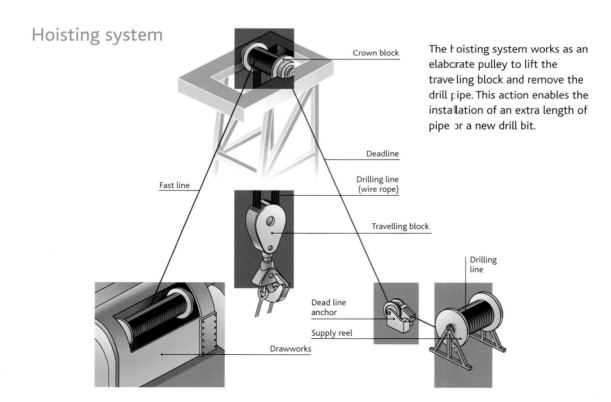

Crown block

Deadline

Drilling line (wire rope)

Fast line

Travelling block

Drilling line

Dead line anchor

Supply reel

Drawworks

©Canadian Centre for Energy Information 2009

Circulating system

A drilling fluid called mud circulates through the drilling bit as it cuts through rock. The fluid lubricates and cools the bit, removes rock cuttings, stabilizes the wall around the hole, and controls the pressure in the wellbore. The mud is a suspension of chemicals and minerals such as bentonite clay in water or sometimes oil. Bentonite is a type of clay that swells when exposed to water.

Workers blend the mixture in the mud-mixing shack. The mud pumps push the fluid up the standpipe and into the drill string through the kelly, in the conventional rig shown on page 51, or through fittings in a top drive mechanism. After passing through the drill bit, the mud and cuttings circulate back to the surface through the space outside the pipe, known as the annulus, and into the mud return line.

The shale shaker, a vibrating screen, then separates the cuttings from the mud. (The well site geologist collects a sample of cuttings from the shale shaker every five metres of well depth.) The cuttings then flow into lined pits or sumps, while the drilling mud flows through the de-sander and de-silter and is recirculated in the mud system. Fluid additives flow through the mixer as the drilling progresses to greater depths. When drilling is completed, the remaining drilling mud is trucked away for disposal or reuse at another site.

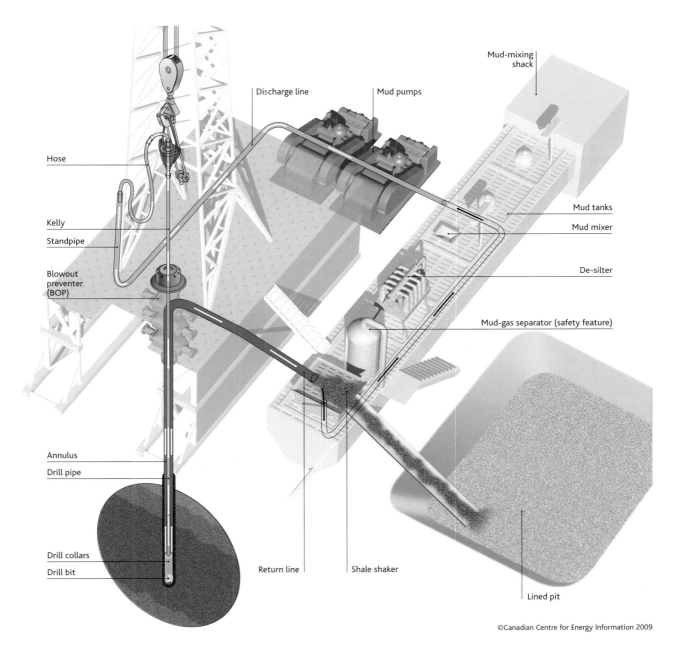

Hose

Kelly

Standpipe

Blowout preventer (BOP)

Annulus

Drill pipe

Drill collars

Drill bit

Return line

Shale shaker

Discharge line

Mud pumps

Mud-mixing shack

Mud tanks

Mud mixer

De-silter

Mud-gas separator (safety feature)

Lined pit

©Canadian Centre for Energy Information 2009

Offshore drilling

The actual drilling mechanism used offshore includes the same components as an onshore rig; however, there are several crucial differences. An offshore rig needs a platform to support it, as land supports the onshore rig. There may be hundreds or thousands of metres of water between the platform and the sea floor. In some offshore operations, it may be necessary to disconnect the rig from the well during drilling, due to storms or icebergs.

The type of platform depends mainly on water depth. In relatively shallow water, the platform can rest its weight on the sea floor. Platforms with retractable legs, known as jack-up rigs, are used for exploration in waters up to 100 metres deep such as those near Sable Island off Nova Scotia. The Hibernia structure on the Grand Banks off Newfoundland and Labrador also rests on the sea floor; it supports crude oil production and

storage as well as drilling rigs for continued development of reservoirs in a radius around the platform.

In deeper water, floating platforms are used. Semi-submersible rigs, raised and lowered by flooding part of the structure, are kept in place by anchors. Semi-submersible rigs are used for most exploration on the Grand Banks off Newfoundland and Labrador. Dynamically positioned drillships and most semi-submersible rigs use propellers and thrusters to maintain position. Drillships are usually employed for drilling in very deep waters. Such drillships were used to drill wells off the East Coast in 2002 and 2003 at a water depth of more than 1,600 metres.

Deepwater drilling is expected to be a significant factor in the future of the oil and gas industry, in Canada and worldwide. Off Nova Scotia, deepwater wells are aiming for natural gas reserves three times larger than those discovered in shallower water on the

Scotian Shelf. Three deepwater wells were drilled on the Scotian Slope by the end of 2002, and two more began drilling in 2003. Two deepwater wells were also drilled off Newfoundland and Labrador in 2003. Drilling activity has slowed since 2003, the peak year for number of wells and metres drilled off the East Coast.

In offshore drilling, a structure called a template is cemented in place on the sea floor to establish a connection between the rig and the wellbore. The template is basically an open steel box with multiple holes in it, depending on the number of wells to be drilled. It contains automatic shutoff valves, called blowout preventers, so that the well can be sealed off if there are problems on the platform or the rig has to be moved. Cables attach the template to floating platforms; the cables are used to position the drill pipe accurately in the template and wellbore, while allowing for some vertical and horizontal movement of the platform.

Federal regulations govern releases of wastes into the marine environment. Low-toxicity drilling fluids are used in offshore drilling. Rock cuttings from drilling with oil-based fluids are either reinjected into wells or are separated from the fluid before they are disposed at sea. Other wastes are taken ashore by service vessels for disposal. Stricter requirements may be imposed in environmentally sensitive offshore areas.

Frontier drilling

Arctic drilling, like offshore drilling, involves the same mechanical components as conventional onshore drilling. Onshore arctic drilling generally takes place in winter when the soil above the permafrost is frozen to provide a firm platform and so roads can be constructed of ice and snow. One recent innovation is a special padding placed between the rig and the ground to insulate the permafrost. Arctic offshore drilling can be done from drillships or reinforced ice islands or, in shallower waters, dredged artificial islands or steel structures filled with dredged material.

Photo courtesy of Hibernia Management and Development Company

Drilling on the Hibernia Platform
Workers handle many kilometres of drill pipe in offshore drilling operations. In 2007 Hibernia project directly employed about 920 people, of whom 91 per cent come from Newfoundland and Labrador.

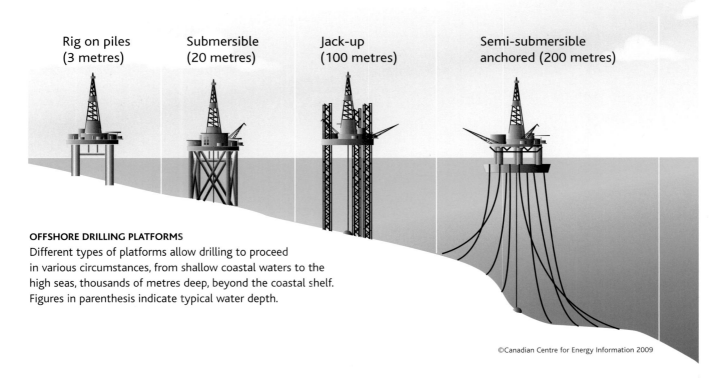

Rig on piles (3 metres)   Submersible (20 metres)   Jack-up (100 metres)   Semi-submersible anchored (200 metres)

OFFSHORE DRILLING PLATFORMS
Different types of platforms allow drilling to proceed in various circumstances, from shallow coastal waters to the high seas, thousands of metres deep, beyond the coastal shelf. Figures in parenthesis indicate typical water depth.

©Canadian Centre for Energy Information 2009

The rigs require additional insulation for arctic operation, and local hunters may be employed to protect crews from polar bears. Companies have established programs to consult with Aboriginal communities and provide jobs, training and business opportunities for Aboriginal people and other residents affected by frontier drilling operations. The National Energy Board and other federal agencies work with territorial authorities and Aboriginal communities to ensure public consultation, local participation and environmental protection in Arctic drilling operations. Environmental assessment and review bodies have been established under Aboriginal land claim agreements.

The growing North American demand for natural gas has prompted increased drilling in the northern territories, mainly in areas close to the Alberta and British Columbia borders where pipelines are in place to carry natural gas to markets in Canada and the United States. Much greater activity is expected if a pipeline is approved to carry natural gas from the Mackenzie Delta to southern markets.

Drilling for crude oil also continues around Norman Wells, which has been connected by pipeline to Alberta since 1985. Meanwhile, the Amauligak field under the Beaufort Sea, discovered in the mid-1980s, remains one of the largest undeveloped conventional oilfields in North America. Further development of Amauligak and other far northern oilfields awaits pipeline or tanker transportation systems to markets.

Similar to offshore authorities, frontier regulators are developing new rules for the disposal of drilling wastes to protect the delicate northern environment. Companies are conducting research into biodegradable drilling fluids and other methods to reduce the volume and toxicity of wastes.

The stages of drilling

Wells are normally drilled in stages, starting with a surface hole drilled to reach a depth anywhere from 60 to 400 metres, depending on underground aquifers and area conditions. The crew then pulls out the drill string and inserts steel pipe, called surface casing, which is cemented in place, to isolate the wellbore from the open hole and the surrounding geological formations. It controls the return flow of mud and other fluids encountered during drilling and also prevents contamination of groundwater.

After setting surface casing and installing the blowout preventers (BOPs), the crew resumes drilling. A probe for shallow gas or heavy oil in eastern Alberta or Saskatchewan may require only two or three days to drill 450 metres through soft shales and sandstone to the target depth. However, a rig may work eight months or longer to penetrate 6,500 metres or more through hard, folded and tilted rocks in the foothills of the Rockies. When the bit needs to be replaced because of wear or changing rock strata, the crew has to pull out the entire string. Sections of pipe have to be unscrewed in single, double or triple sections, depending on the height of the derrick, and stacked upright in the derrick. The whole string then has to be put back into the hole again, with the new bit in place. This process, which can be very laborious and time-consuming for a deep hole, is called tripping. Tripping may also be necessary to place special equipment or remove obstructions. At each stage, additional casing is inserted to isolate the wellbore from the walls of the open hole.

Major improvements in the durability of bits and the formulation of drilling fluids since the 1980s have greatly reduced the number of trips required to drill a well. Shallow wells today are often drilled without a bit change. Yet another recent innovation, drilling with casing, can eliminate even more steps in the drilling process. In this method, casing pipe is used instead of conventional drilling pipe, and remote controls permit the downhole assembly to be detached and raised on a cable inside the casing. The well is drilled and

Air and underbalanced drilling

Occasionally, wells are drilled without mud to increase penetration rates and to avoid sensitive rock formations coming into contact with water. In air drilling, compressed air removes the cuttings. Drillers can also obtain many of the same benefits through underbalanced drilling — using mud lightened by the addition of nitrogen or other gas.

Underbalanced drilling has become increasingly common in Western Canada because it minimizes damage to the producing reservoir. This is especially useful in clay formations. Clays can collapse into the wellbore or swell if water-based drilling fluids are used. Underbalanced drilling minimizes the seepage of the drilling fluid into the reservoir and allows crude oil and natural gas to be produced more effectively.

A disadvantage of underbalanced drilling is that some natural gas may be released while drilling proceeds. In the past, this gas would have been burned in a flare or incinerator at the wellsite. Companies, government regulators and nearby residents today seek to minimize prolonged flaring. If possible, the natural gas is shipped by pipeline to a processing plant.

cased simultaneously. This method has been used to set surface casing and to drill wells all the way to target depth. It can reduce or eliminate the need for tripping, and can reduce the time to drill a well by more than 20 per cent.

If the string breaks, a specialist is called in to catch and retrieve the "fish" with special tools. No one wants to lose an expensive bit and bottom-hole assembly, but the blocked hole is the real problem. As a last resort, the crew drills a curved section called a sidetrack to bypass the problem area.

New drilling techniques

Due to increasing concern about land use and environmental disturbance, directional wells are often used for infill drilling. In contrast to traditional vertical wells, directional wells use a slanted or curved (deviated) wellbore. More than one directional well can be drilled from a common drilling pad.

Horizontal drilling, which extends the wellbore into a much larger portion of the oil-bearing formation, has been employed since the late 1980s to improve production and enhance recovery. Horizontal drilling increases production rates by contacting more of the reservoir. This increases oil recovery and may reduce the amount of water and natural gas mixed with the crude oil.

New drilling techniques also make it possible to drill a number of horizontal offshoots or laterals from a single vertical, directional or horizontal wellbore. This is called multiple entry and has proved useful in many types of crude oil and natural gas formations.

Coiled tubing

Coiled tubing has been an important recent innovation in well completion and servicing. Coiled tubing is a continuous, jointless, high-pressure-rated hollow steel tube or pipe that is

brought to the wellsite or offshore drilling platform on reels of up to 9,000 metres. It can be used in place of conventional production tubing, which is made of joined sections of pipe and is similar to a drill string. Special equipment is used to insert the coiled tubing through the wellhead into the wellbore. This method is considerably quicker and more efficient than joining sections of pipe.

Coiled tubing has proved useful in applications such as well stimulation and underbalanced drilling. It can also be used with downhole motors, driven by mud circulation, for certain kinds of drilling such as drilling horizontal wells from existing vertical wells. On the Hibernia platform off Newfoundland and Labrador, for example, coiled tubing is used for a variety of drilling, completion and servicing tasks.

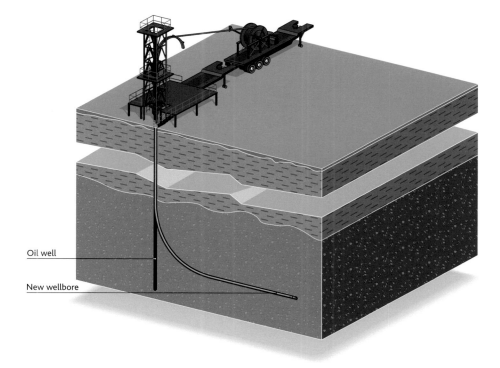

Oil well

New wellbore

COILED TUBING FOR DRILLING
The use of coiled tubing, a continuous length of flexible steel pipe, allows horizontal drilling from existing vertical wells. The bit is turned by a hydraulic mud motor on the downhole end of the tubing. As a result, horizontal operations from an existing wellbore become cost-effective and minimize disturbance to the environment. Coiled tubing is also used for many other applications during well completion and servicing.

©Canadian Centre for Energy Information 2009

Specialized jobs

The supervisor is known as the rig manager or "toolpusher." Crews include drillers, derrickmen (who maintain pumps and mud system), motormen (who maintain motors), floorhands and leasehands. In addition to managing drill bits and pipe, derrickmen operate the drilling-fluid circulation system, maintain the machinery and perform various specialized tasks. A wellsite geologist monitors well cuttings, examines cores and identifies potential reservoirs. The rigs operate around the clock, seven days a week, and the crews typically work 12-hour shifts for two weeks and then have a week off. The workers sometimes live on-site in a temporary camp.

LAND-BASED RIG PERSONNEL
About 75 workers employed to drill one well, four to seven at the rig at one time, number can vary depending on type of well drilled

Company representative	Rig manager (toolpusher)	Driller	Drilling crew (derrick, motor, mud, floor lease hands)	Mechanic/ electrician

Covers company interests, plans strategy, orders needed supplies and equipment, makes on-site decisions.

Lives on-site, works closely with company representative and crew for on-site decisions.

Supervises drill crew.

Crew of three to six – handles mud, drill pipe, casing and rig maintenance; erect and dismantle rig.

Either two or three crews in rotating shifts (tours) – operate 24 hours a day, seven days a week; size of crew determined by size of rig or operation.

Maintains engines, compressors and electrical equipment (usually present on large rigs and in remote locations).

OFFSHORE RIG PERSONNEL
65 – 70 workers on the platform at one time, plus another 50 or so working directly for the operator

Offshore installation manager	Rig manager (toolpusher)	Driller/assistant driller	Drilling crew (derrickman, pumpman, floorman, motorman and roustabout)	Subsea supervisor/ subsea assistant	Mechanical crew (maintenance supervisor, chief engineer mechanical supervisor, chief mechanic, motorman and rig mechanic)	Electrical crew (electrical supervisor, chief electrician, electrician and electronic technician)

Manages rig personnel and resources.

Supervises drilling operations and associated activities; plans and schedules drilling.

Operate drilling and mud circulating equipment.

Crew of 16 handles mud mixing and pumping systems, casing, drill pipe and rig maintenance.

Maintain and repair subsea systems and associated surface equipment.

Crew of six maintains and repairs mechanical and rig equipment.

Crew of five installs, maintains and repairs rig electrical equipment.

OFFSHORE SUPPORT WORKERS

Drilling and support services
Geologist logging specialist, drilling superintendent (company man)

Marine department
Barge supervisor/assistant, barge supervisor, ballast control (stability) operator/assistant, ballast control operator, able-bodied seaman, paint foreman/painters, marine mechanic, crane operator/assistant, crane operator, welder

Catering and housekeeping

Supply
Helicopter crew, supply boat personnel (captain, mate, able-bodied seaman and materialsman)

Other support workers
Management, accounting and administration, materials coordinator, health, safety and environment coordinator

©Canadian Centre for Energy Information 2009

Well control

The drill bit may be several kilometres deep by the time high-pressure hydrocarbon deposits are reached. Adding heavy minerals such as barite (barium sulphate mineral) to the mixture can increase the weight of the drilling fluid. Drillers adjust the weight so the mud is heavy enough to hold back formation fluids from entering the hole, but not so heavy that the mud will penetrate into the reservoir and damage it.

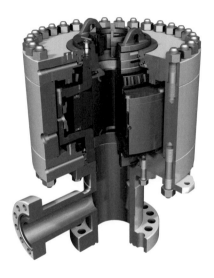

BLOWOUT PREVENTERS
Blowout preventer (BOP) devices are typically installed on the top of the casing, below the rig floor. BOPs are large valves that help control the liquid and gas pressure in the well. One type of BOP can seal off the annulus, the space between the drill pipe and the casing, if the drill pipe is still in the hole. Another can shear off the drill pipe and thus seal off the entire well, while a third can seal off the well if no drill pipe is in the hole. Several of these BOPs are mounted together, and this assembly is known as the BOP stack.

Illustration courtesy of Northland Energy Corporation/ Precision Drilling

If the formation pressure is higher than the pressure exerted by the mud column, formation fluid may enter the wellbore. This is known as a kick and must be controlled to prevent a blowout. Kicks are detected by sensitive instruments that monitor the mud flow and composition and the mud tank levels. Drillers control most kicks simply by managing the mud flow and increasing the weight of the mud.

If drillers cannot control the pressure in a well, this can result in a blowout or uncontrolled release. Today, blowouts are extremely rare, and nearly all wells are completed without incident. Blowouts waste valuable resources and often damage the environment. Also, some may release foul-smelling sour gas containing toxic hydrogen sulphide, which is a major hazard for workers, nearby populations and the environment.

Blowouts can be enormously expensive to bring under control. Sometimes a second well has to be drilled to relieve the pressure on the damaged well. Rig crews are trained to use blowout preventers and drilling fluid to reduce the frequency and severity of blowouts.

Logging and coring

Logging operations obtain information about rock formations. Logging can be conducted in an open or cased hole.

Logging is performed by lowering a package of instruments, called wireline logging tools, into the wellbore. The instruments record and transmit information about the rock layers' thickness, porosity and permeability and the composition of fluids such as crude oil, natural gas or water contained in them.

A logging instrument can also be mounted on the string above the bit to send information continuously during drilling. It sends signals to the surface

by means of pulses, like sonar signals, in the mud. Another instrument, the measurement-while-drilling (MWD) tool, can similarly measure the direction and precise location of the bit. MWD is particularly useful while drilling horizontal wells.

If more information is needed about the rocks, a special cylindrical bit may be used to cut a core sample for analysis by geologists and other specialists such as reservoir engineers, geochemists and palynologists.

Drillstem testing

A common way to determine potential crude oil or natural gas production is the drillstem test, which uses a special tool in place of the bit on the end of the string. The tool has valves and rubber sleeves, called packers, that can be controlled from the surface. First, the packers are expanded to isolate the section of the hole to be tested. Next, valves on the tool are opened, allowing liquids or gas from the formation to flow into the empty drill pipe. This gives a good indication of the type and volume of the fluids in the formation, their pressure and rate of flow.

What happens if crude oil or natural gas is found?

Completion is the procedure by which a successful well is readied for production. The first step for most wells in Canada is the installation of production casing.

The casing – tubular steel pipe connected by threads and couplings – lines the total length of the wellbore to ensure safe control of production, to prevent water entering the wellbore and to keep rock formations from sloughing into the wellbore. Production casing is set in place by pumping a cement mixture into the casing and forcing the cement back up the annulus (the space between the casing and wellbore). The task must be done quickly but carefully, because a poor cement job can adversely affect the producing formation.

Once the cement has set, the drilling rig is usually moved from an onshore well site, and a smaller, truck-mounted service rig is brought in to complete the well. (For offshore wells, the completion is done from the drilling rig.) There were about 1,068 service rigs in Canada in 2008. Service rigs also return to wells periodically to perform maintenance, replace equipment or enhance production.

The second step is the installation of the production tubing. Production tubing is steel pipe smaller in diameter than the production casing. It is lowered into the casing and held in place by packers that also isolate the producing layers of rock. The tubing hangs from a surface installation called

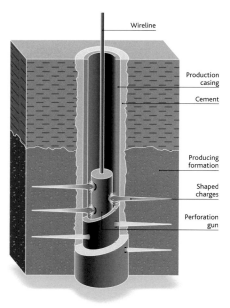

PERFORATION
The perforation charge penetrates through the production casing and about 30 centimetres into the producing formation.

©Canadian Centre for Energy Information 2009

the wellhead. The wellhead includes valves, chokes and pressure gauges that make it possible to regulate production from the well.

Perforation

The other step is to perforate the well. The casing prevents the hole from collapsing, but it also prevents the crude oil or natural gas from entering the wellbore. Therefore, holes are made through the casing and into the formation. Perforation is usually accomplished with an explosive device that is lowered into the well on an electrical wireline to the required depth. This device, a collection of explosive charges in a special carrier, is called a perforating gun. An electrical impulse fires the charges to perforate the casing, surrounding cement and reservoir rock.

Abandonment and reclamation

If the well is a dry hole, not capable of producing commercial quantities of crude oil and natural gas, the drilling crew plugs the wellbore with cement and cleans up the site. A similar procedure is followed if a mature producing well is no longer economical to operate.

The cost of abandonment and cleanup is a significant factor in an oil company's planning. Environmental regulations ensure the company remains responsible for the site until government authorities issue a reclamation certificate. It can take years to complete the reclamation. Plans for decommissioning and reclamation are developed in consultation with landowners and other affected parties.

In older producing areas of Western Canada, there are many "orphan" wells where the original owner has gone out

of business or cannot be determined. Some of these wells were not properly reclaimed or subsequently developed problems such as crude oil or natural gas leaking through the casing or cement. Operating companies now pay into a fund controlled by government agencies that undertake the necessary repairs and cleanups. Government regulations and computerized records help to reduce the future likelihood of orphan wells. Some jurisdictions require a reclamation bond be posted before an initial licence is granted.

In offshore areas, an abandonment plan must be submitted and approved along with the licence application. Regulations require that abandonment take place without creating hazards to navigation or the environment.

Success

Of the 20,203 wells drilled in Canada in 2008, only 1,689 were abandoned as non-commercial "dry holes" – a success rate that reflects the sophistication of modern exploration methods, the continual increase in geologic knowledge about the main petroleum-producing regions, and the larger proportion of development wells compared to exploratory wells. The success rate is much lower in offshore areas because fewer wells have been drilled and basic geological knowledge is still being accumulated. Of the successful wells, 4,845 were completed as crude oil-producing wells and 12,951 were completed as natural gas-producing. The next chapter explains how conventional crude oil and natural gas are produced, and how hydrocarbons are extracted from other sources such as oil sands and coal seams.

Flaring – an important safety procedure

Flaring is the burning of natural gas that cannot be economically processed or sold. It can be an important safety procedure for preventing the accumulation of dangerous concentrations of gases, especially at facilities that handle sour gas. The hydrogen sulphide (H_2S) in sour gas must be flared because it is toxic and heavier than air. Flaring converts the H_2S into sulphur dioxide (SO_2) that is dispersed in the plume of hot gases from the flare. Flaring is done in compliance with government air quality standards.

The continuous small flame visible at some oil and gas facilities is not a flare but a pilot light, fed by sweet natural gas. It remains lit to assure instantaneous combustion of any gas release.

In recent years, industry and government actions have reduced the amount of flaring. Flaring not only wastes a valuable resource, it releases greenhouse gases into the atmosphere. Incomplete combustion can release carbon monoxide, unburned hydrocarbons, soot and ash, and toxic substances such as volatile organic compounds, polycyclic aromomatic hydrocarbons and various sulphur compounds. Flaring is also a common reason for public complaints about odours, smoke and noise.

The flaring of solution gas – natural gas produced along with crude oil – has been a major target for reduction. In Alberta, for example, solution gas had accounted for about three-quarters of the flaring in the province. From 1996 to 2007, the volume of solution gas flared in Alberta was reduced by 76 per cent; this was significantly greater than the 50 per cent reduction goal established by government and industry. The proportion of solution gas recovered, processed and marketed in Alberta increased from 87.7 per cent in 1988 to 95.8 per cent in 2007.

The petroleum industry now uses a variety of strategies to reduce flaring. Where volumes are sufficient to recover natural gas economically, it is gathered and pipelined to processing facilities. In recent years, some companies have also started to re-inject gas underground. Changes in procedures and equipment in natural gas operations reduce the need for flaring during maintenance. New methods also reduce the duration of flaring at new wells. If there are nearby pipelines to processing plants, the test gas can be connected to the system rather than being flared.

Another recently introduced technology uses small gas-fired generators to produce electricity from gas that would otherwise be flared. Research is also under way to develop more efficient flare and incinerator designs that improve efficiency and reduce emissions in situations where flaring cannot be avoided.

Learn More

The Centre for Energy's *Sour Gas and Flaring Questions + Answers* focuses on the questions Canadians living in close proximity to sour gas operations have about this issue. Free to download and purchase in quantity at **www.centreforenergy.com/ Education/Bookstore**

Hydrogen sulphide

Hydrogen sulphide (H_2S) is a toxic gas formed by the breakdown of organic materials. It can be found in natural gas, crude oil, sewage, swamps and stockyards and in the processing of pulp and paper. The gas is colourless, but the "rotten egg" smell is evident even at low concentrations. Natural gas and crude oil containing H_2S are termed "sour." About one-third of the natural gas produced in Western Canada is sour.

At higher concentrations, H_2S stops people and animals from breathing, and if not handled properly, it can be deadly. Because H_2S is heavier than air, it tends to accumulate in low-lying areas.

Critical sour gas wells are wells with the potential for large H_2S releases or for any release that can affect population centres. Any well that can release gas containing more than two cubic metres per second of H_2S during the drilling stage is a critical sour gas well. In designating critical sour gas wells, regulators also consider population density, the environment, the sensitivity of the area, and the expected complexities during the drilling phase.

Most such wells are located in the western half of Alberta and in northeastern British Columbia. Special precautions are taken during drilling critical sour gas wells. These include specific requirements for drilling plans and procedures, well design, specialized worker training and supervision, safety specialists, detailed emergency response plans and associated community consultation. Regulations also specify standards for equipment such as blowout preventers (BOPs), mud-gas separators, drill pipe and valves.

When the drill bit enters the critical zone in a well where sour gas is likely to be encountered, additional precautions include providing continuous gas "sniffing" or testing, supplying breathing apparatuses for rig personnel, and notifying people living nearby.

Companies and governments have developed computer models to predict how sour gas would disperse in the event of a blowout or other accidental release. Emergency response planning for sour gas wells is based on the results of these models. Plans specify steps that would be taken to protect people's health and safety in the event of a release. The measures might include igniting the gas, which converts H_2S into sulphur dioxide (SO_2). Sulphur dioxide is also toxic but disperses more effectively because heat carries it upward, resulting in lower ground-level concentrations.

One of the first activities initiated in a sour gas blowout is the monitoring of air quality downwind from the well. Mobile equipment is set up to track the plume and to identify concentrations of gas both inside and outside the emergency planning zone. If the emergency response team determines that there is a danger, residents will be evacuated or the well ignited to protect the public.

Safety and environmental protection

To ensure safety and reduce environmental impacts, government authorities enforce strict environmental and equipment standards and operating procedures on rigs. In developing regulations, the government consults with industry bodies such as the Canadian Association of Oilwell Drilling Contractors and the Canadian Association of Petroleum Producers.

The industry is addressing the environmental impacts of drilling. For example, companies use new techniques to reduce the production of waste fluids from drilling, to lessen the toxicity of drilling fluids and to improve the disposal of waste fluids. Better planning also reduces the surface disturbance caused by drilling, and new standards are in place for site reclamation.

The challenge

The challenge in production is to get as much crude oil and natural gas out of the ground as possible, at the lowest cost and with the fewest effects on the environment.

Production – recovering resources

After drilling has located a reservoir of crude oil or natural gas, the operating company's production department takes over the task of bringing the resource to the surface. Petroleum is not produced from underground lakes. Rather, crude oil and natural gas are contained in the pores and fractures of certain sedimentary rocks in the same way that water is held in a sponge.

In a mature producing area such as Western Canada, recovering more crude oil and natural gas from old wells is an important job. Getting the most petroleum, at the least cost, is also a key challenge in new production areas such as East Coast offshore projects.

The vast hydrocarbon deposits of the Alberta oil sands pose additional, unique problems for scientists and engineers as they seek more efficient and economical ways to recover the tar-like bitumen. According to the National Energy Board, oil sands could provide as much as 90 per cent of Canadian crude oil production by 2030.

A greater proportion of Canadian natural gas production has been coming from deeper wells in more remote areas, as well as from wells off Nova Scotia. Several projects are under way to develop production of natural gas trapped in coal deposits in Alberta, and similar methods may eventually be used on coal seams in other parts of Canada.

Producing crude oil and natural gas

Natural gas generally flows to the wellbore under its own pressure. As a result, most natural gas wells are equipped only with chokes and valves to control the flow through the wellhead into a pipeline. When wellhead pressure is less than the pipeline pressure, a compressor is installed to boost the low-pressure natural gas into the pipeline.

The production of crude oil is more complicated than production of natural gas. Crude oil has larger molecules and moves through rocks less easily. The percentage of the oil in the reservoir that can be produced naturally, called the recovery factor, is determined by a large number of variables. These include the weight of the oil, the viscosity (how sticky it is), the porosity and permeability of the rock, the pressure in the oil reservoir, and the pressure of other fluids such as natural gas and water in the reservoir.

Hundreds of businesses

Thousands of Canadians are employed in crude oil and natural gas production jobs ranging from reservoir engineering to oilfield operations and well servicing. Hundreds of businesses provide services to support the drilling and production sectors. Many of these companies are members of the Petroleum Services Association of Canada.

The top priority in recent years has been to make production as efficient as possible. This is necessary because finding and operating costs in Canada have been relatively high compared to other countries' costs.

One measure of success is that total Canadian crude oil production did not decline, as was predicted in the 1970s and 1980s, but actually increased in the 1990s and 2000s to reach record annual levels of more than 190 million cubic metres (including natural gas liquids and oil sands) in every year since 1997. Natural gas output also increased substantially, reaching a record total of 180 billion cubic metres in 2001, then falling to 175 million cubic metres in 2007.

These production increases were largely due to stepped-up exploration and development of natural gas, improved technology such as horizontal drilling and expanded oil sands mining and steam-injection projects.

Pumping

While some oil wells contain enough pressure initially to push crude oil to the surface, eventually all oil wells drilled today require pumping. This is also known as artificial lift.

If a well requires it, a pump is lowered down the tubing to the bottom of the well on a string of steel rods, referred to as the rod string. The rod string is hung from the wellhead and connected to a drive unit and motor on the surface. The rod string conveys power to the pump either by rotating or moving up and down, depending on the type of pump employed. The traditional "iron horse" pumpjack is a familiar sight in oil-producing areas. Submersible pumps are used on some wells. Progressive cavity pumps, a type of screw pump, are also used on some oil wells.

Photo courtesy of Petroleum Industry Training Service

Service Rig
Truck-mounted service rigs are used to complete wells, install equipment, perform maintenance and enhance recovery. Service rigs can even perform some drilling tasks by using downhole mud motors to turn the drill bit.

Careers in energy

Service rigs and specialist contractors perform regular maintenance on wells. Well servicing is a significant source of employment in petroleum-producing regions, and Canadian servicing equipment and expertise have found markets around the world.

Learn more about careers in energy at **www.centreforenergy.com**

Stimulation

In many crude oil and natural gas wells, one additional step is required – stimulating the formation by physical or chemical means so that hydrocarbons can move more easily to the wellbore through the pores or fractures in the reservoir. This is usually done before installing a pump or when the pump is removed for maintenance.

One form of stimulation is acidizing – the injection of acids under pressure into the rock formation through the production tubing and perforations. Hydrochloric acid, for example, is particularly effective in dissolving portions of limestone and dolomite formations. This creates channels beyond the perforations for crude oil and natural gas to flow back to the well. Acidizing is often followed by fracturing.

Fracturing or fracing is another common method of stimulation. A fluid such as water or an oil product is pumped down the hole under sufficient pressure to create cracks (fractures) in the formation. Proppant – a hard substance such as sand, ceramics or resin-coated material – is injected with the fluid. As the fluid disperses, the material remains to prop open the fracture.

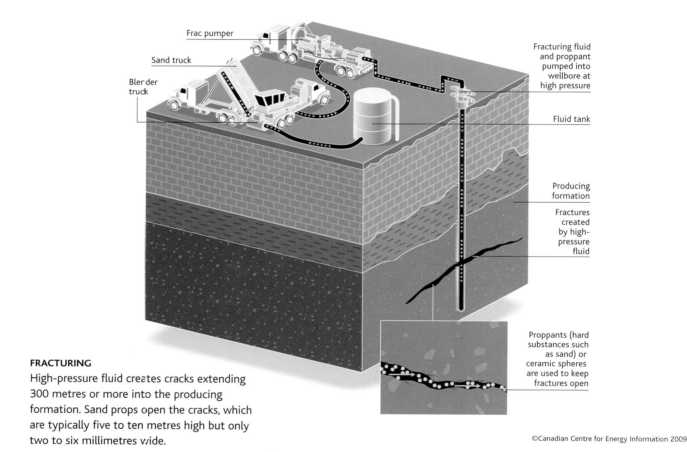

Frac pumper

Sand truck

Blender truck

Fracturing fluid and proppant pumped into wellbore at high pressure

Fluid tank

Producing formation

Fractures created by high-pressure fluid

Proppants (hard substances such as sand) or ceramic spheres are used to keep fractures open

FRACTURING
High-pressure fluid creates cracks extending 300 metres or more into the producing formation. Sand props open the cracks, which are typically five to ten metres high but only two to six millimetres wide.

©Canadian Centre for Energy Information 2009

Unconventional natural gas

Natural gas from coal

Natural gas from coal (NGC), also known as coalbed methane, is simply the natural gas formed and trapped in coal beds. NGC is generated during the coalification process that transforms organic material such as peat bogs into coal.

Exploration and development of NGC has been ongoing in the United States since the 1970s, but did not get underway in Canada until the mid-1990s. Despite the drilling of more than 140 wells in the 1990s, successful production was not achieved until 2000. Since then, more than 19,000 wells have been drilled and re-completed, and production for 2008 was about 8.0 million cubic metres.

In coal seams, the methane can occur as "dry" gas or be associated with saltwater or freshwater. The most common production method uses wells drilled into the naturally fractured coal seams. Dry gas can be produced like conventional natural gas. If the gas is associated with water, the wells initially remove water from the coal, but

eventually methane is freed from the coal as the pressure and surface tension are lowered. The disadvantage is the long time period before significant gas production begins and the need to dispose of the water, usually by injection into deep wells beneath existing groundwater aquifers. Researchers are investigating other means of freeing the methane from the coal, including the injection of carbon dioxide, which could also provide a way to reduce greenhouse gas emissions.

Gas hydrates

Researchers in Canada, Japan and elsewhere are testing possible methods to recover methane from hydrates – crystals of water and methane molecules – found in vast quantities on ocean floors and in the Arctic. According to the U.S. Geological Survey, the worldwide amounts of carbon bound in gas hydrates is conservatively estimated to total twice the amount of carbon to be found in

all known fossil fuels on Earth. However, no economical method has yet been found to produce natural gas from hydrates.

Since 1998, industry and government scientists have been assessing gas hydrates in the Canadian Arctic. A $27-million research program in 2002 and 2003 involved three wells at a depth of 1,150 metres in the Mackenzie Delta 120 kilometres north of Inuvik. The experiments generated gas flows using three production methods: heating the hydrates, lowering pressures in the formations, and injecting substances such as methanol. The scientists noted that much more research and development will be needed before natural gas production from hydrates can be considered practical and economical on a commercial scale.

The challenge

As an almost pure form of natural gas found in coal deposits, production of natural gas from coal could have important implications for the petroleum industry. The challenge will be to overcome environmental and technical obstacles to make this resource a feasible and economical energy resource.

NATURAL GAS FROM COAL RESOURCES
(billions of cubic metres)

Region	In-situ	Recoverable Resource Low	Recoverable Resource Ref	Recoverable Resource High
Western Plains				
Alberta and Saskatchewan	9,696.40	313.60	627.20	1,058.40
Northeast British Columbia Plains	700.00	0.00	17.50	35.00
Rocky Mountain Foothills and Front Ranges				
Northeast British Columbia	1,680.00	0.00	42.00	84.00
Northern Alberta	414.40	0.00	10.36	20.72
Central Alberta	453.60	0.00	11.34	22.68
Southern Alberta	226.80	0.00	5.60	11.20
Southeast British Columbia	394.80	0.00	9.80	19.60
Other British Columbia				
Vancouver Island	32.48	0.00	0.81	1.62
Intermontagne	250.60	0.00	3.46	6.92
East Coast				
Sydney	27.44	0.00	0.34	0.67
Pictou	0.78	0.00	0.20	0.39
Cumberland	11.76	0.00	0.29	0.59
Total	**13,889.06**	**313.60**	**728.90**	**1,261.79**

Source: Canadian Gas Potential Committee

Hibernia

The $5.8-billion Hibernia project began producing crude oil off Newfoundland in November 1997. Natural gas produced along with the oil provides energy for the platform, with the excess reinjected into the producing formation.

Photo courtesy of Hibernia Management and Development Company

Shale gas

Shale gas is conventional natural gas that is produced from reservoirs predominantly composed of shale with lesser amounts of other fine-grained rocks rather than from more conventional sandstone or limestone reservoirs.

The gas shales are often both the source rocks and the reservoir for the natural gas, which is stored in three ways:

- adsorbed onto insoluble organic matter called kerogen
- trapped in the pore spaces of the fine-grained sediments interbedded with the shale
- confined in fractures within the shale itself

Producing gas from shale usually involves horizontal drilling to expose as much of the reservoir to the well bore as possible, and fracture stimulating the reservoir. Fracturing may be necessary multiple times during the productive life of the well.

Shale gas is being actively explored in northeast British Columbia, west-central Alberta, central and south-central Saskatchewan, southwest Ontario and along the St. Lawrence River in Quebec.

Oil recovery methods

In primary recovery – the initial approach to producing oil – natural reservoir pressure or simple mechanical pumps are used to raise oil to the surface. Most oil wells drilled in Canada today have to be pumped. Primary recovery rates can range from 0.5 per cent to 60 per cent of the resource in the reservoir, depending on the combination of crude oil and rock characteristics. The average primary recovery rate is less than 20 per cent. This means that a lot of oil would usually be left in the reservoir.

A number of methods can improve primary recovery. The most common is infill drilling, which involves drilling more wells into the same pool so the oil does not have to travel as far through the rock to reach a wellbore.

Enhanced recovery

Further crude oil production can be obtained by injecting water ("waterflooding") or natural gas to maintain reservoir pressure and push oil out of the rock. This is called secondary recovery. More advanced methods are referred to as tertiary recovery.

The most common tertiary recovery method for light and medium crude oil is miscible flooding. In this procedure, natural gas liquids (ethane, propane and butane) are injected into special injection wells. When dissolved, these liquids reduce the surface tension and viscosity to help release the oil from the reservoir rock. Carbon dioxide has also been used to a limited extent in Canada for miscible floods. This has the added advantage of using a greenhouse gas that would otherwise be released into the atmosphere. Two such projects are operating in Alberta and Saskatchewan, and several more are in the planning stage. However, some reservoirs are more amenable to this technique than others. Research is continuing on the injection of carbon dioxide into underground formations; another possible use is to stimulate production of natural gas from coal deposits.

In heavy oil and in-situ bitumen production, enhanced recovery generally involves the application of heat, most commonly by steam injection. Major improvements in heavy oil and bitumen recovery have been achieved by steam-assisted gravity drainage (SAGD), which uses parallel pairs of horizontal wells for steam injection and oil recovery.

Even with all these techniques, the average recovery in the conventional oilfields is seldom more than 30 per cent of the original oil. The remaining resource represents billions of cubic metres of oil that has been discovered in Canada but cannot be produced economically with existing technology.

The principal method for maintaining or increasing natural gas production in Canada has been regular servicing, including acidizing and/or fracturing. The campaign to reduce flaring and venting since the mid-1990s has also led to more capture of marketable natural gas.

Well maintenance

Crude oil and natural gas wells are like motor vehicles; they require periodic maintenance for best performance. Many problems can develop over the life of a well. Silt or wax can build up, slowing or halting the flow of hydrocarbons. The walls of the hole can start to cave in. Scale can accumulate in tubing. Corrosion or flaws in the cement can also cause leakage. Pumps on crude oil wells also need periodic "tune-ups."

Frontier and offshore petroleum

The development of frontier and offshore petroleum resources was delayed for many years by the high cost and environmental issues involved in building production and transportation systems.

The major exception is Norman Wells in the Northwest Territories, which has been producing since the 1920s. It differs from other frontier operations because it is part of the Western Canada Sedimentary Basin and is connected by a pipeline to Alberta and other markets. A feature of Norman Wells is the use of directionally drilled wells and artificial islands to reach the large part of the reservoir located under the Mackenzie River. Exploration activity has also occurred in the southern Northwest Territories near areas connected by pipeline to markets.

The first modern frontier production was crude oil from the Bent Horn well in the Arctic Islands. From 1985 to 1996, tankers carried crude oil from Bent Horn to East Coast ports during the short summer shipping season. Except for seasonal tanker shipments such as those from Bent Horn, no major crude oil production is expected from the Arctic until a pipeline is built from the Mackenzie Delta to southern Canada.

In 1999, natural gas production began in the Mackenzie Delta to supply the community of Inuvik, but major natural gas development also awaits construction of pipelines to southern markets. Four major oil and gas companies and an Aboriginal partnership have proposed a 1,300-kilometre natural gas pipeline along the Mackenzie River Valley to southern Canada; a preliminary information package for the project was submitted to federal and territorial authorities in June 2003. Project proponents filed an environmental impact statement in October 2004. Prior to that, in August 2004, a joint

review panel was appointed as an independent body with a mandate "to evaluate the potential impacts of the project on the environment and the lives of the people in the project area." From 2005 through 2007, the panel held a total of 115 hearing days, collected more than 5,000 written submissions and received thousands of recommendations. The panel's final report will be released in December 2009.

Crude oil was produced between 1992 and 1999 from the Panuke and Cohasset fields 250 kilometres off Nova Scotia. The project produced up to 6,350 cubic metres per day of light, sweet (low-sulphur) crude oil.

The $5.8-billion Hibernia project, 315 kilometres off Newfoundland and Labrador, began oil production in 1997. Initial production of nearly 10,000 cubic metres per day increased to more than 20,000 cubic metres per day in 2002, peaking at 32,475 in 2004. In 2008, Hibernia production averaged 22,100 cubic metres per day.

The Sable Offshore Energy Project began producing natural gas in 1999 for shipment through a subsea pipeline system to Nova Scotia. Initial processing of the natural gas occurs offshore, and natural gas liquids are removed at a plant in Goldboro, Nova Scotia. The 13 million cubic metres of natural gas per day are then shipped by pipeline to markets in the Maritime provinces and New England. Additional discoveries of natural gas off Nova Scotia may be connected later to the Sable processing and pipeline systems or may require their own facilities.

The Terra Nova project began crude oil production in 2002 from a floating production facility on the Grand Banks 350 kilometres off Newfoundland and Labrador. Since inception, except for 2006 when the wells were shut in for more than five months, production has

averaged 17,650 cubic metres per day. The field has an expected production life of 15 to 17 years, compared with 20 years or more for Hibernia.

In 2002, Husky Energy Inc. and Petro-Canada announced their intention to proceed with the White Rose project, another floating production facility on an oil and gas field 350 kilometres east of St. John's. Crude oil production from White Rose began in 2005 and has since averaged 16,250 cubic metres per day.

The latest project on the East Coast is the Deep Panuke gas pool, located on the Scotian Shelf, about 250 kilometres southeast of Nova Scotia. Regulatory approvals were finalized in 2007, and first production is expected in 2010. Production rates are forecast at 8.5 million cubic metres per day and the reserve life is estimated to be 13 years.

Additional crude oil production from these fields or elsewhere in the Jeanne d'Arc Basin, likely using floating production facilities, is expected as exploration and development proceed on other fields. Some fields may use common facilities for oil processing, storage and tanker loading.

Technologies currently being used for crude oil and natural gas production in very deep waters in the Gulf of Mexico and elsewhere around the world are being examined for possible adaptation to produce deepwater resources off Canada's East Coast. Exploration is now moving into deeper water off both Nova Scotia and Newfoundland and Labrador.

Despite the difficulties posed by arctic and offshore conditions, the operation and completion of frontier wells includes the same basic steps used for onshore wells. Horizontal, directional and multiple-entry techniques allow wells to reach large areas of the producing formations.

Offshore oil facilities have injection wells to return produced water and natural gas to the formations. This disposes of byproducts without affecting the environment and also maintains pressure in the reservoirs. Offshore projects also use part of the produced natural gas to meet energy requirements on the platforms.

Terra Nova, White Rose and Hebron

The $2.8 billion Terra Nova project began production in 2002, and has a maximum approved production rate of 28,620 cubic metres of crude oil per day. The field has an expected production life of 15 to 17 years, compared with 20 years or more for Hibernia.

The White Rose project began production in 2005 and output averaged 16,000 cubic metres per day in 2008.

Partners reached agreement with the Newfoundland and Labrador government in 2008 to proceed with development of the Hebron heavy oil field, with first production expected between 2016 and 2018.

Learn More

The Centre for Energy's *Canada's Evolving Offshore Oil and Gas Industry* explores East Coast offshore activity as well as recent developments in British Columbia and the Arctic. Free to download and purchase in quantity at **www.centreforenergy.com/ Education/Bookstore**

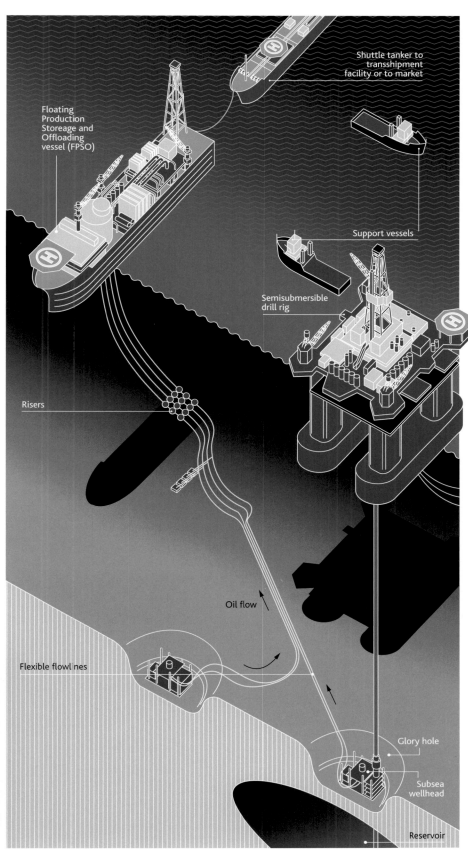

Shuttle tanker to transshipment facility or to market

Floating Production Storeage and Offloading vessel (FPSO)

Support vessels

Semisubmersible drill rig

Risers

Flexible flowlines

Oil flow

Glory hole

Subsea wellhead

Reservoir

©Canadian Centre for Energy Information 2009

The marine environment

East Coast crude oil and natural gas fields are located in historically important fishery areas. Industry and regulators scrutinize plans and operations to minimize the possibility that crude oil and other contaminants will be released into the marine environment. Cold water temperatures and frequent storms would make it difficult to clean up spills. Low temperatures also slow down the processes of evaporation and bacterial action that eventually break down crude oil.

Many technologies developed for the equally sensitive waters of the North Sea are proving useful as exploration and development proceed on the East Coast. Examples include new drilling fluids with reduced impact on the environment, and better treatment methods for drill cuttings and produced water.

The Canadian industry has been a leader in developing emergency response plans for spills from oil tankers. The industry continues to improve its ability to respond by learning from incidents in other parts of the world.

Tanker-leasing practices now involve intense scrutiny of vessels and staff. New tankers include the latest safety features such as double hulls and advanced navigation systems. The tankers transporting crude oil from the Grand Banks off Newfoundland and Labrador are double-hulled and specially designed for the icy, stormy waters of the area.

In addition, a network of regional marine spill response centres is continually being upgraded. Under the Canada Shipping Act, all marine shippers and receivers of petroleum products must belong to spill response organizations.

Ontario's offshore

Natural gas has been produced from offshore facilities on the Ontario side of Lake Erie since the 1960s. Ships and barges are used during ice-free months to drill wells and service the wellheads and pipelines on the lake floor. A jackup rig, originally used for drilling, has been converted into a seasonal field compressor to boost pressure in a portion of the 1,500 kilometres of pipelines carrying natural gas to onshore processing facilities. Water depths are generally less than 30 metres. Although the volumes are small, the production from the 550 offshore wells in Lake Erie is profitable because it is located close to markets. Environmental regulations do not allow offshore drilling for crude oil in the Great Lakes. However, directional and horizontal wells drilled from onshore tap crude oil reservoirs several kilometres out under Lake Erie.

THE SABLE OFFSHORE ENERGY PROJECT
The $2-billion Sable Offshore Energy Project includes offshore natural gas production facilities, a subsea pipeline, onshore gas processing facilities and a pipeline across Nova Scotia and New Brunswick to the northeastern United States. Production began in 1999.

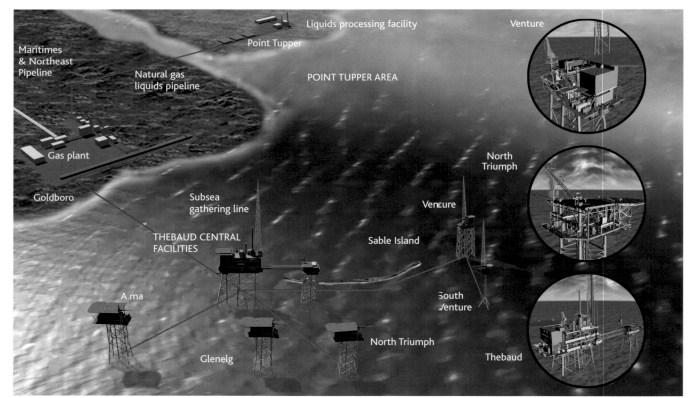

Source: Sable Offshore Energy Inc.

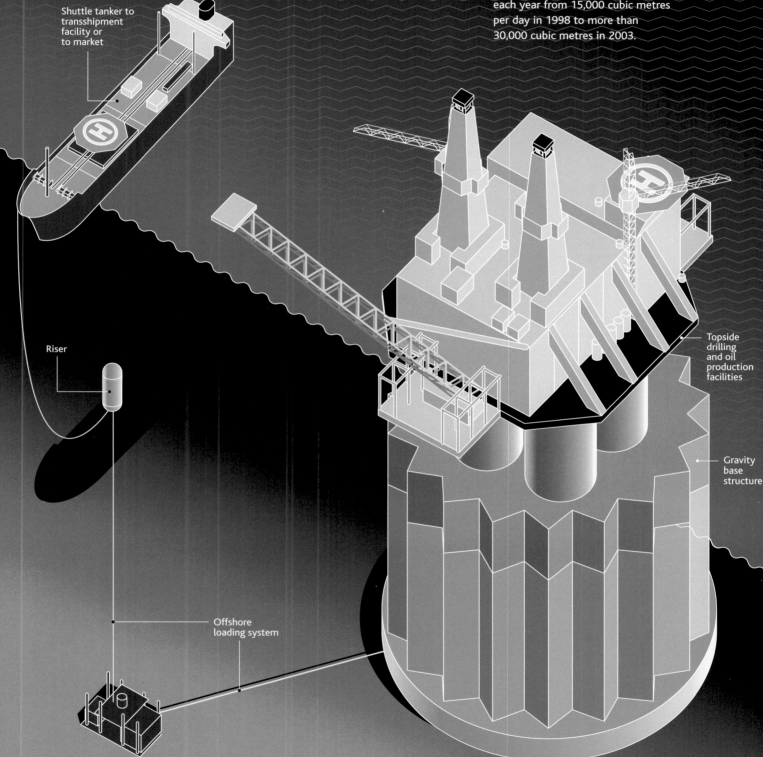

Hibernia Energy Project

The Hibernia project, 315 kilometres, east-southeast of St. John's, Newfoundland and Labrador, began oil production in 1997. Production rose each year from 15,000 cubic metres per day in 1998 to more than 30,000 cubic metres in 2003.

Shuttle tanker to transshipment facility or to market

Riser

Offshore loading system

Topside drilling and oil production facilities

Gravity base structure

©Canadian Centre for Energy Information 2009

Mining and in-situ bitumen

The tar-like bitumen in the oil sands of northern Alberta is the world's largest known petroleum resource. However, the viscous substance is too thick to flow through rocks, wellbores and pipelines. Many technological and economic challenges have to be overcome in order to produce and transport bitumen and to process it into desirable products such as gasoline and diesel fuel.

Oil sands accounted for 35 per cent of Canada's crude oil production in 2003, and could provide more than 53 per cent by 2010 if development continues at the current pace and conventional light oil production continues to decline.

By the end of 2008, investment in the oil sands included $40.5 billion in projects under construction and more than $100 billion in proposed projects. These projects will continue to stimulate numerous employment opportunities in everything from construction to plant operation and

the many related businesses providing goods and services to the projects. The activity has attracted workers from across Canada and provided training, jobs and business opportunities for Aboriginal people and other local residents.

Companies have also taken many steps to create opportunities for local businesses, including many enterprises owned and operated by Aboriginal people. Splitting contracts into many components makes it possible for smaller companies to bid on them. Oil sands developers use open house events, local media and ongoing consultation to ensure that local people are aware of upcoming business opportunities.

Aboriginal people make up about 12 to 15 per cent of the population in the Athabasca oil sands area, and industry has made a concerted effort to provide opportunities for them. In 2002, the two operating mining projects employed about 700 Aboriginal people,

and almost as many worked for contractors supplying goods and services to the projects. (Syncrude Canada Ltd. is the largest industrial employer of Aboriginal people in Canada.) About $2.6 billion worth of contracts were awarded to local Aboriginal companies between 1996 and 2007 – $606 million in 2007 alone. Companies planning new projects consult routinely with Aboriginal communities to ensure that they benefit from oil sands development. Extensive scholarship and training programs are available for Aboriginal people in the region.

Significant labour shortages in the oil sands industry were predicted in a 2003 study conducted by the Petroleum Human Resources Council of Canada. The study indicates 8,000 new positions will be created as production increases over the next decade. Heavy equipment operators, process operators, heavy duty mechanics and power engineers will be

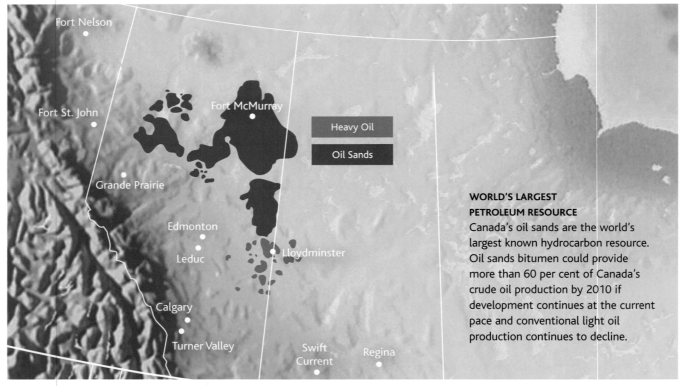

Heavy Oil

Oil Sands

WORLD'S LARGEST PETROLEUM RESOURCE
Canada's oil sands are the world's largest known hydrocarbon resource. Oil sands bitumen could provide more than 60 per cent of Canada's crude oil production by 2010 if development continues at the current pace and conventional light oil production continues to decline.

©Canadian Centre for Energy Information 2009

Typical oil sands mining operation

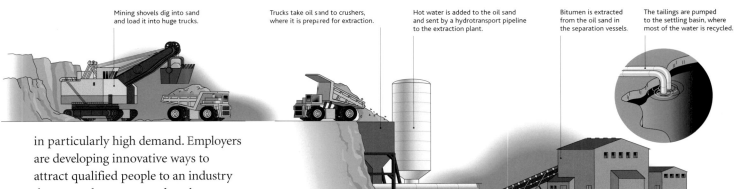

Mining shovels dig into sand and load it into huge trucks.

Trucks take oil sand to crushers, where it is prepared for extraction.

Hot water is added to the oil sand and sent by a hydrotransport pipeline to the extraction plant.

Bitumen is extracted from the oil sand in the separation vessels.

The tailings are pumped to the settling basin, where most of the water is recycled.

©Canadian Centre for Energy Information 2009

in particularly high demand. Employers are developing innovative ways to attract qualified people to an industry that must also accommodate the impending retirement of an aging first generation workforce.

To meet the need for highly skilled labour, the oil sands companies work with educational institutions and government agencies to provide training for existing employees and prospective workers. Keyano College in Fort McMurray is now the centre for training in the specialized skills used in oil sands mining and upgrading. It also has links to schools in the Aboriginal communities of Fort Chipewyan, Fort McKay and Janvier. In addition, the companies offer extensive in-house training and work-sharing programs. One result of these initiatives is that many women now work in non-traditional roles such as heavy-equipment operation.

The population of Fort McMurray, the centre of the Athabasca oil sands industry, reached 47,240 in 2002 with another 11,000 in the surrounding areas of the Regional Municipality of Wood Buffalo. Rapid growth continued and by

the end of 2007, the population had increased to 65,400 in Fort McMurray and 23,767 in the surrounding area. Multi-stakeholder groups co-ordinate planning for community and regional needs such as transportation, housing, services, education, labour supply, environmental protection and recreation. For example, the thousands of workers needed during project construction are housed in permanent work camps on the project sites to lessen the strain on local housing and services.

The effect of oil sands and heavy oil development is also evident in the Cold Lake area of Alberta, whose population of 25,000 includes a number of Aboriginal communities. As in the Fort McMurray area, companies co-ordinate their activities and create opportunities for local businesses and Aboriginal people.

The benefits of oil sands development extend to those parts of Canada that provide steel, machinery, and other goods and services. In fact, it has been estimated that about 60 per cent of oil sands capital investment is actually spent outside Alberta. One study indicates that $30 billion in investment would create about 19,000 permanent new jobs in Alberta and another 28,000 in other provinces.

As the technologies for producing oil sands bitumen have improved, the environmental effects per cubic metre have been reduced. From 1990 to 2004, for example, the greenhouse gas emissions to produce a cubic metre of synthetic crude oil dropped by about 27 per cent, and further improvements are expected to reduce this an additional 20 per cent by 2010. A 2003 study indicated that the total greenhouse gas emissions, including those from final consumption, were about 10 per cent greater for fuels produced from bitumen compared to fuels produced from conventional crude oil.

Oil sands mining projects

Oil sands mining projects have three main functions – mining the resource, separating the bitumen from the sand, and upgrading the bitumen into a marketable commodity. It takes about six cubic metres of mined oil sand to produce a cubic metre of synthetic crude oil.

Mineable bitumen deposits are located near the surface and can be recovered by open-pit mining techniques. The Syncrude Canada Ltd. and Suncor Energy Inc. oil sands projects near Fort McMurray initially used huge, specially designed excavators (drag-lines and

Learn More

The Centre for Energy's *Canada's Oil Sands* explains the increasing importance of oil sands to Canadians. Free to download and purchase in quantity at **www.centreforenergy.com/ Education/Bookstore**

bucketwheels) to mine the oil sand, which was then carried to the plant by conveyor belts. This system was expensive to operate and maintain, especially during the winter.

New truck-and-shovel mining methods introduced in the 1990s considerably improved efficiency and reduced the cost. Along with higher crude oil prices and changes in tax and royalty regimes, the improved methods paved the way for multi-billion-dollar expansions of the existing projects plus proposals for additional mining projects.

The new methods use hydraulic and electrically powered shovels to scoop up the oil sand and load it into enormous trucks that can carry more than 400 tonnes at a time. The trucks dump their loads into a machine that breaks up lumps and removes rocks from the sand, then mixes it with water to create a slurry carried by pipeline to the processing plant.

This slurry-pipelining system, called hydrotransport, eliminates the need for long conveyor belts and also begins the process of separating the bitumen from sand, water and minerals. In the plant,

a hot water process completes the separation of the bitumen. Hydrotransport reduces the cost, energy requirements and land disturbance by oil sands mining projects.

In oil sands mining, clean sand from the processing facility is returned to mined-out areas. Fast-growing grass – using species native to the area wherever possible – stabilizes the surface of the reclaimed land, and some of this land is replanted with trees. In one research project, wood bison now graze on reclaimed land following oil sands mining.

Water quality

While both mining and in-situ bitumen operations use large quantities of water, most of that water can be and is recycled. The impact that oil sands mine tailings have on water quality does not lend itself to such easy solutions.

In the extraction process at mining projects, the water picks up tiny particles of clay. Ponds are used to hold the resulting mixture of clay and water. Oil sands developers have found several methods of managing these mixtures, known as tailings. If a layer of fresh water is placed over the tailings, for example, this "water cap" can function as a normal aquatic ecosystem while the clay particles slowly drift to the bottom.

Newer technologies avoid this long settling time by not using caustic soda in the extraction process. As a result, the clay particles settle more quickly to the bottom. Another new technology, known as consolidated tailings, uses gypsum to solidify the tailings. Yet another proposed method would thicken the tailings into a thick paste, requiring less area for disposal than watery tailings. Some companies plan to use several methods to reclaim sites once their operations cease. Because there is still some debate about whether the tailings ponds can become biologically productive ecosystems over the long term, developers are continuing to study the matter.

In-situ projects have made a continuing effort to reduce water use through increased recycling. Developers have also been devising methods of using brackish (slightly salty) water from underground aquifers to meet part of their water needs.

Another issue for in-situ operations is the possibility that casing failures in steaming operations could contaminate drinking water supplies in underground aquifers. In the Cold Lake area, investigations of the impacts of casing failures on groundwater quality found the effects were restricted to the immediate vicinity of a casing failure. Produced fluids released into an aquifer from a casing failure are recovered by pumping back the released fluids. A number of improvements have also been made to the design and operation of in-situ oil well casings. These improvements are intended to reduce the number of future casing failures and minimize their consequences. For example, by detecting breaks earlier, when they are the size of pinholes, the amount of fluid that may be released into a groundwater aquifer is significantly reduced.

In the late 1990s, an extensive investigation of groundwater quality around in-situ heavy oil operations was conducted near Cold Lake. The study found that regional groundwater quality had not been affected by in-situ heavy oil operations. The study also recommended that the monitoring of groundwater quality be enhanced. Since then, groundwater monitoring and research programs have been implemented, and this work continues. Preliminary laboratory and field experiments to date have yielded no data to indicate that regional groundwater quality in the Cold Lake area has deteriorated over time.

In-situ bitumen recovery

In-situ production methods are used on bitumen deposits buried too deep for mining. These techniques can include steam injection, solvent injection and firefloods in which oxygen is injected and part of the resource burned to provide heat. To date, steam injection has been the preferred method.

Imperial Oil Limited's Cold Lake project is Canada's largest in-situ bitumen recovery project. The underground oil sands reservoir is heated with steam. This softens the semi-solid bitumen and separates it from the accompanying sand. Imperial's recovery method is called cyclic steam injection. The bitumen is then pumped to the surface and diluted with condensate (pentanes and heavier liquid hydrocarbons obtained from natural gas production) for shipping by pipeline. Several other companies operate large in-situ projects, and more are planned.

Horizontal drilling increases the production per well considerably in some heavy oil and bitumen formations, but the technology is not economical for all types of reservoirs. Steam assisted gravity drainage (SAGD), using parallel pairs of horizontal wells to inject steam and remove bitumen, has become the preferred technology for in-situ production from suitable reservoirs. The SAGD process is also applicable to smaller scale developments as well as large ones. The disadvantage of SAGD is that it requires large amounts of energy, water and water treatment.

Vapour extraction (VAPEX) is an alternative method that uses natural gas liquids such as propane and butane instead of steam to free bitumen from sand. Like SAGD, VAPEX uses parallel horizontal wells to inject the solvent liquids and extract the bitumen. A project near Fort McMurray is testing the commercial feasibility of VAPEX. Although VAPEX is less energy-intensive than SAGD, research indicates production rates are also lower. In addition, hybrid steam-solvent processes are currently under development for reservoirs in which steam or solvent processes alone are not suitable.

STEAM ASSISTED GRAVITY DRAINAGE (SAGD)

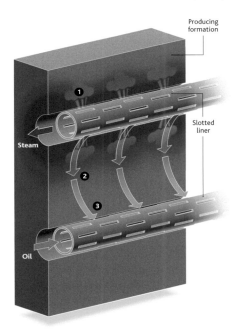

Producing formation

Slotted liner

Steam

Oil

❶ Steam is injected into oil-producing reservoir

❷ As the steam permeates the sand, the oil is heated and becomes less viscous

❸ The oil flows more freely through the slotted liner and is pumped to the surface

CYCLIC STEAM STIMULATION
Steam saturates the oil sands formation, softening and diluting the bitumen so it can flow to the well during the production phase.

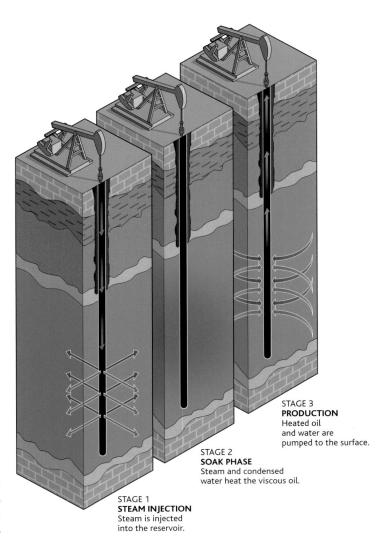

STAGE 3
PRODUCTION
Heated oil and water are pumped to the surface.

STAGE 2
SOAK PHASE
Steam and condensed water heat the viscous oil.

STAGE 1
STEAM INJECTION
Steam is injected into the reservoir.

©Canadian Centre for Energy Information 2009

Photo courtesy of Shell Canada

Processing – making marketable commodities

The challenge

Oil and gas processing aims to separate petroleum into marketable commodities and remove undesirable substances as safely and cost-efficiently as possible with the least possible effect on the environment.

Petroleum reserves are created over millions of years by complex chemical and biological processes under particular conditions of temperature and pressure. Each petroleum reservoir produces a unique mixture of hydrocarbons and other substances. Processing facilities separate the marketable commodities from these mixtures.

Most crude oil and natural gas production requires some processing to remove undesirable components before the commodity goes to market. Some processing facilities are basically just settling tanks for removing sand and water, while others are multi-million-dollar plants treating large volumes of sour gas or bitumen.

Elemental Sulphur

Canada is the world's largest producer and exporter of elemental sulphur, which is used for making fertilizers, pharmaceuticals and other products. The sulphur is typically stored in blocks (above) and shipped in pellet form (left).

Photo courtesy of Shell Canada

Processing facilities separate the raw petroleum into the major products sold by the upstream sector:

- crude oil, a mixture of liquid hydrocarbons
- market-ready natural gas, composed mainly of methane, the simplest hydrocarbon molecule
- natural gas liquids (NGLs), the heavier gaseous hydrocarbons, including ethane, propane and butane
- condensate (pentanes and heavier liquid hydrocarbons) obtained from processing natural gas for market, and
- sulphur, obtained from processing natural gas and transported by truck or train as liquid, pellets or slabs.

About two-thirds of Canada's petroleum production does not require extensive processing before it can be shipped by pipeline. Relatively simple field facilities remove sand and water from the petroleum stream and separate it into crude oil, natural gas and NGLs. Operating such facilities is a major part of the work for field personnel in production firms.

Most field processing uses well-established techniques and equipment common to oil and gas operations around the world. However, engineers and scientists have developed unique methods to process Canada's large endowments of sour gas and bitumen safely and efficiently, with minimal environmental impact. Canadians are international industry leaders in these areas and sell large amounts of equipment, training and consulting services in foreign markets.

Thousands of Canadians work in gas-processing facilities and in plants that purify raw natural gas and upgrade heavy oil and oil sands bitumen. The facilities are located as close as possible to the production sites, and they generate considerable economic activity in many areas of Western Canada. Offshore production facilities also include processing equipment to remove water and NGLs from natural gas streams and to separate water and natural gas from crude oil.

Natural gas processing

The natural gas purchased by consumers consists almost entirely of methane, the simplest hydrocarbon. In gas reservoirs, however, methane is typically found in mixtures with heavier hydrocarbons – such as ethane, propane, butane and pentanes – as well as water vapour, hydrogen sulphide (H_2S), carbon dioxide, nitrogen and other gases.

Almost all of these substances are removed from the gas stream at processing plants located near production areas or at "straddle plants" located on major pipeline systems.

Of the nearly 600 natural gas processing plants in Alberta, more than 60 are large facilities that produce elemental sulphur as a byproduct of the H_2S in sour gas. The others handle sweet gas or small volumes of H_2S, which is flared, incinerated or reinjected back into a reservoir. There are about 9,000 kilometres of pipelines in Alberta carrying sour gas from roughly 4,000 producing sour gas wells.

STAGES OF NATURAL GAS PROCESSING
Natural gas is not usually marketable as it comes from the wellhead. The gas often contains a mixture of contaminants such as shale, sand, water, carbon dioxide or hydrogen sulphide that are removed as the natural gas goes through various stages of processing before becoming marketable.

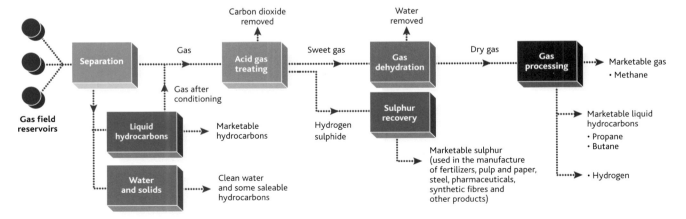

©Canadian Centre for Energy Information 2009

The British Columbia sour gas industry includes three large sulphur-recovery plants, four smaller field plants and more than 5,000 kilometres of sour gas pipelines. In addition, smaller volumes of sour gas are produced and processed in the Northwest Territories, Saskatchewan, Manitoba and Ontario. The Deep Panuke discovery off Nova Scotia also contains hydrogen sulphide, which could be removed from the gas stream and injected into a deep geological formation. Gas re-injection is also being examined in other areas as a means of meeting air quality requirements and reducing greenhouse gas emissions.

Removing liquids and sulphur

The raw natural gas from wellheads may pass through compressors to maintain or increase pressure and may be heated to prevent freezing and condensation. Glycol dehydrators are typically used to remove water from natural gas streams, although the industry has been developing alternative technologies because of concern about emissions of benzene, toluene, ethylbenzene and xylenes (BTEX) from these facilities. Industry associations have developed best practices guidelines to reduce emissions from the more than 4,000 glycol dehydrators in Canada, and as a result benzene emissions from glycol dehydrators were reduced 76 per cent between 1995 and 2002.

In the processing plants, gas is chilled to separate the natural gas liquids from methane. Then H_2S is removed by a chemical reaction in the presence of catalysts. The natural gas emerging from the plants meets pipeline specifications for dry gas, but may still contain natural gas liquids, which are removed at straddle plants on main transmission pipelines.

Natural gas liquids are sold separately and used for enhanced oil recovery, as raw materials for oil refineries or petrochemical plants, or as fuels.

Condensate (a mixture of pentanes and heavier hydrocarbons) is used as a diluent to reduce the viscosity of heavy oil and bitumen so they can be shipped through pipelines; refineries then use the condensate as feedstock along with the bitumen or heavy oil.

Most of the H_2S recovered at gas plants is converted into elemental sulphur. Sulphur is used in fertilizer manufacture and other industries, but a prolonged oversupply on international markets has led to growing stockpiles of sulphur in Western Canada. The cost of transportation to potential buyers is often higher than the market price. Other possible uses include construction materials and pavement.

Acidic water runoff from sulphur stockpiles is neutralized in holding ponds and must meet government standards before being released into the environment. Sulphur storage facilities are lined and enclosed by barriers to prevent acidic water from leaching heavy metals out of soil and contaminating groundwater.

Sulphur dioxide

Since the 1950s, concerns have been voiced about the possible environmental and health effects of sulphur dioxide emissions. These emissions, which contribute to acidic rain or snow, are produced by coal-fired power plants, oil sands upgrading and other industrial processes as well as by sour gas processing and sour gas flaring. Governments regulate sulphur dioxide emissions through plant licencing specifications and ambient air quality standards.

Natural gas processing contributes almost half the sulphur dioxide emissions in Alberta. Oil sands facilities and power plants are also major sources, as are oil refineries, pulp and paper mills and fertilizer plants. Oil sands operators have made major cuts in sulphur dioxide emissions, which have declined to 453 kilotonnes in 2005 from 608 kilotonnes in 1995, even though synthetic crude oil production has increased.

Sour gas processing and bitumen upgrading account for a substantial portion of Alberta's relatively high per capita emissions of SO_2. These processes reduce the emissions from use of petroleum in consuming areas and remove toxic hydrogen sulphide from the natural gas going to market. Refining low-sulphur synthetic crude oil results in less air pollution around oil refineries and reduces sulphur emissions from gasoline and diesel engines. Switching to natural gas reduces the acid rain effects from coal-fired energy use across North America.

Fluid containment

In addition to crude oil and water, the petroleum industry handles many other liquids — drilling fluids, fuel, lubricants, solvents and various chemicals — that can contaminate water if improperly released into the environment. Wherever possible, the industry reduces the volume and toxicity of liquids used in operations. New regulations and industry practices are improving the containment of such liquids. Double-walled fuel storage tanks and walled concrete pads for chemical drums are examples of improved containment. Based on extensive research and design, new regulations detail the procedures and criteria for management of oilfield waste.

Crude oil processing

Conventional crude oil is initially processed at field facilities called batteries. The main component of a battery is one or more tanks in which saltwater and sand sink to the bottom and natural gas bubbles off the top. Clean oil collects in the middle. The water is reinjected into the producing formation to help maintain reservoir pressure, and sand is collected for disposal in an approved landfill. The natural gas, known as associated gas or solution gas, is directed to processing plants if feasible. Otherwise, the gas is flared or incinerated if quantities are too small to justify recovery. (Incineration is combustion in a closed vessel under controlled conditions.) Since 1988, there has been a sharp reduction in the proportion of solution gas flared. This has been done to conserve valuable product and to reduce air emissions. No producer wants to flare natural gas if there is an economic way to use it.

Upgrading heavy oil and bitumen

Since most refineries in Canada were designed to process conventional light crude oils, Canada's increasing production of heavy oil and bitumen has created a challenge. One solution is to upgrade the heavy compounds to create synthetic crude oil (a mixture of hydrocarbons similar to a light crude oil). Synthetic crude oil is usually quite low in sulphur and contains no residue or very heavy components. Upgrading can occur at or near the producing area or the refinery.

Bitumen and some heavy oils are too viscous to flow through pipelines, so they must be diluted. Condensates, liquids obtained from natural gas, have been used as the diluent (20 – 30 per cent of the blended volume) for most such pipeline shipments in Canada. Due to Western Canada's rising natural gas production through the 1990s, the supply of condensate was sufficient to meet the diluent requirement, but there was concern that condensate supplies could decline in the future while bitumen production continued to increase. The locations of upgrading facilities were determined in part by the cost and availability of condensates. Since then, however, shippers have found that synthetic crude oil can be used as an effective diluent, and conventional light crude oil or refined petroleum products can also be used for this purpose. Venezuela ships very heavy crude oil in a water emulsion.

At the heart of the problem is the high proportion of large, carbon-rich molecules in heavy oil and bitumen – which are sometimes called hydrogen-poor petroleum resources.

CRUDE OIL BATTERY
Crude oil is processed initially at field facilities called batteries.

©Canadian Centre for Energy Information 2009

BITUMEN UPGRADING

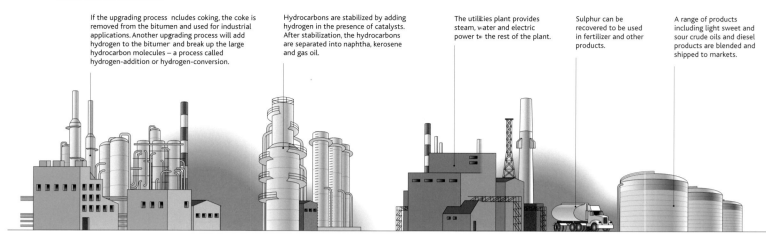

If the upgrading process includes coking, the coke is removed from the bitumen and used for industrial applications. Another upgrading process will add hydrogen to the bitumen and break up the large hydrocarbon molecules – a process called hydrogen-addition or hydrogen-conversion.

Hydrocarbons are stabilized by adding hydrogen in the presence of catalysts. After stabilization, the hydrocarbons are separated into naphtha, kerosene and gas oil.

The utilities plant provides steam, water and electric power to the rest of the plant.

Sulphur can be recovered to be used in fertilizer and other products.

A range of products including light sweet and sour crude oils and diesel products are blended and shipped to markets.

©Canadian Centre for Energy Information 2009

The process

Upgrading involves the use of temperature, pressure and catalysts to crack the big molecules into smaller ones. Adding hydrogen and/or removing carbon then creates hydrocarbon molecules like those in lighter oil. The product of upgrading, known as synthetic crude oil or upgraded crude oil, is a blend of naphtha and distillates that can be used by many refineries as a replacement for conventional light crude oil to make gasoline, diesel, jet fuel and heating oil. Most synthetic crude oils are "sweet" (low in sulphur).

Upgrading is usually a two-stage process. In the first stage, coking or hydrocracking, or both, are used to break up the molecules. The coking process removes carbon, while hydrocracking adds hydrogen. In the second stage, a process called hydrotreating is used to stabilize the products and to remove impurities such as sulphur. The hydrogen used for hydrocracking and hydrotreating is manufactured from natural gas and steam. The by-product of the coking process is carbon (coke), which may be sold separately or stockpiled.

Upgrading produces three main products: naphtha, kerosene and gas oil. (Naphtha is a light petroleum component used mainly to make gasoline. Gas oil is a type of fuel oil, somewhat heavier than kerosene.) These can be blended together into a custom-made crude oil equivalent, or they can be sold or used separately. The Syncrude and Suncor oil sands projects use some of their production to fuel the diesel engines in trucks and other equipment in their operations.

Shell Canada is using a new upgrading technology called hydrogen addition at an upgrader next to Shell's refinery at Scotford, Alberta. The technology produces a range of low-sulphur synthetic crude oils for use at Scotford or other refineries. The upgrader began processing diluted bitumen shipped from the Albian Sands Muskeg River Mine in April 2003.

The facilities

Some north-central U.S. refineries have added upgrading facilities to handle Canadian heavy oil directly. This is a practical option if there is an adequate supply of condensate for diluting the oil, and pipeline capacity to bring the oil to the refineries. Some eastern Canadian refineries can also process shipments of heavy oil, usually delivered by tanker from abroad. The NewGrade Upgrader facility in Regina, which began upgrading heavy oil in 1990, sends most of its synthetic crude to an adjacent refinery.

The other alternative is to upgrade the product at the upstream end of the pipeline. Both the Syncrude Canada and Suncor Energy oil sands projects have large upgraders to convert bitumen into high-quality, low-sulphur synthetic crude. The Suncor plant also produces other products such as diesel fuel. The Husky Energy Lloydminster Upgrader in Saskatchewan began processing Alberta and Saskatchewan bitumen and heavy oil in 1992.

Major increases in the capacity of the Fort McMurray and Lloydminster upgraders are planned. This will double their total capacity, from about 65,000 cubic metres per day in 1997 to more than 130,000 cubic metres per day in 2008.

Albian Sands' Muskeg River Mine ships up to 34,000 cubic metres of diluted bitumen through a 450-kilometre pipeline to the upgrader that has been added to Shell Canada's refinery in Scotford, Alberta.

Companies have proposed building at least two more upgraders in the Fort McMurray area by 2010, and additional volumes of bitumen could be processed by existing upgraders or upgrading facilities added to refineries in the Edmonton area.

Spills

The upstream petroleum industry routinely handles huge volumes of liquids, considerably larger than the 410 million litres of crude oil and natural gas liquids shipped to customers every day. In some older oilfields, more than 20 litres of saltwater are produced for every litre of crude oil. This saltwater is separated from the oil at processing facilities and re-injected underground into the oil-producing rock formation. Where companies draw from local water resources, they are required to obtain licences for water use; water is a natural resource regulated by the government.

Corrosion in oilfield pipelines carrying mixtures of crude oil and saltwater is the most common reason for upstream spills. The industry addresses this problem by stepping up inspection and maintenance of facilities, installing new computer technology to detect leaks, and replacing or relining sections of pipeline. The Alberta Energy Resources Conservation Board, which regulates more than 80 per cent of Canadian crude oil and natural gas production, has identified spill prevention as a major target for enforcement efforts. Facilities that fail to meet standards are shut down. Other jurisdictions have adopted similar regulations.

When a spill threatens surface water – streams, rivers or lakes – industry crews are dispatched immediately to halt the leakage and prevent the contamination from spreading. Industry co-operatives in each producing area maintain stockpiles of absorbent booms, temporary dams, special boats and equipment for this purpose. They conduct regular training exercises using vegetable oil and natural dye to practise skills and test equipment. Industry and government officials test water quality downstream from spills to make sure that water meets federal and provincial standards. After the initial cleanup, crews remove contaminated soil and vegetation from the banks for disposal by incineration or landfilling. Reclamation of the site then begins.

A large portion of oil spilled on land will eventually evaporate or be consumed by natural microbial action, a process that can be speeded up by tilling and fertilizing the soil. The oil industry traditionally has used this method of "land farming" on the majority of spills. High-temperature kilns are sometimes used to remove oil contamination from soil. In other instances, the soil is excavated and trucked to an approved industrial landfill site lined with plastic and/or clay. A new technology, currently being developed and tested by the industry, uses underground pipes and barriers to direct underground water flows into channels where bacteria degrade the hydrocarbons.

Careers in energy

Among the careers available in petroleum processing are chemical engineering technologists, customer support analysts, database analysts, engineering geologists, environmental engineers, gas fitters, legal secretaries, materials engineering technologists, mineral processing engineers, mining engineers, mining engineering technologists, pipefitters, process engineers and software application and data processing systems specialists.

Learn more about careers in energy at **www.centreforenergy.com**

Freshwater resources

Oil sands mining projects use water to transport and process bitumen. Heavy oil projects use water to generate steam. Many oil and gas facilities use water for cooling or during processing. Government authorities regulate water use to prevent unacceptable environmental impacts. This issue is commonly addressed by greater recycling of water used in facilities. Some operations reduce water use even while substantially increasing production. One option under study is greater use of brackish (slightly salty) water from underground aquifers or even the saltwater produced along with crude oil, to replace current uses of drinkable groundwater and surface water. Impacts on water resources are among the factors considered by regulators in deciding whether to approve a new facility or expansion.

Photo courtesy of TransCanada Pipelines

The challenge

Transportation systems must provide safe, reliable and efficient movement of crude oil, natural gas, natural gas liquids and refined oil products from where they are produced to where they are consumed. They aim to do this as safely and economically as possible while minimizing effects on the environment.

Transportation – moving and selling crude oil and natural gas

Canada's crude oil and natural gas resources are located mainly in rural and remote areas of Western Canada, the Arctic and offshore. Consumers are concentrated in urban centres across southern Canada and the United States. Transporting petroleum from producers to consumers is a large and vital part of the oil and gas industry.

Almost all of Canada's crude oil and natural gas production is transported invisibly through a vast network of pipelines buried more than a metre underground. Crude oil, natural gas liquids and refined products are also transported by tanker, barge, railway and truck. Pipelines are the only method used to deliver natural gas in Canada today. Elsewhere in the world, specially designed tankers carry liquefied natural gas (LNG) from production facilities to markets. Nova Scotia, New Brunswick and Quebec have been suggested as possible locations for new LNG terminals that would then transport the natural gas by pipeline to customers in the Maritimes and New England.

The invisible highway

Supply and demand are linked together in Canada by about 700,000 kilometres of pipelines – long enough to circle the Earth 17 times at the equator. Some are massive steel conduits more than a metre in diameter, while others are plastic tubes just a few centimetres wide. They form delivery systems as vast and complex as Canada's railroads, highways or electric transmission lines.

Did you know?

Devices used to clean and inspect the insides of pipelines are called "pigs" because the early models reportedly squealed like a piglet as they moved through the pipe. Pigs originally were just cleaning devices, with scrapers to remove wax buildup, but electronic devices were later added to create "smart pigs" for pipeline inspection.

Careers in energy

Careers in the petroleum transportation sector include commercial divers, control centre operators, drafting technologists, environmental toxicologists, facilities engineers, gas plant operators, geomatics and surveying engineers and technologists, hazardous waste management technologists, truck drivers, logistics specialists, heavy duty mechanics, heavy equipment operators, helicopter and small aircraft pilots, pipefitters, pipeline integrity engineers, regulatory affairs advisors, resource engineers, risk analysts, safety officers, welders and more.

Learn more about careers in energy at **www.centreforenergy.com**

Pipelines fall into four categories:

- flowlines or gathering lines move crude oil and natural gas and combinations of these products from wellheads to oil batteries and natural gas processing facilities
- feeder lines transport crude oil and other products such as natural gas liquids from batteries, processing facilities and storage tanks in the field to the long-distance haulers of the pipelines industry, the transmission pipelines
- transmission pipelines are the main conduits for transporting crude oil and natural gas within a province and across provincial or international boundaries, and
- local distribution companies or provincial co-operatives operate natural gas distribution lines that deliver natural gas to homes, businesses and some industries.

According to the Canadian Energy Pipeline Association, about 24,000 Canadians are directly or indirectly employed by operations involving transmission pipelines. About 12,400 people work for gas distribution utilities. All pipelines pay property taxes to local governments. Transmission pipeline operators pay more than $320 million annually in property taxes to local governments across Canada.

Storage

The transportation sector includes large storage facilities for crude oil, refined oil products, natural gas and natural gas liquids. These facilities are often situated at both the upstream and downstream ends of pipeline systems, and sometimes at locations in between. They enable transmission companies to manage the flow through their pipelines, meet demand in the winter heating season ("buffering") and provide orderly delivery of commodities to customers.

Crude oil and refined oil products are usually stored in large above-ground tanks. The tanks may have floating roofs or geodesic domes to prevent evaporation and the buildup of gases in the tanks. Berms lined with low-permeability materials such as clay, plastic, asphalt and/or concrete surround liquid storage facilities to contain any spills or leaks.

Natural gas is stored in underground salt caverns or depleted natural gas fields. Natural gas liquids can be stored in cylindrical or spherical tanks, but larger volumes are also stored in underground salt caverns. During offshore production, crude oil is stored in a fixed platform on a floating production, storage and offloading vessel. The crude oil is then transferred to double-hulled tankers for shipment to terminals in Canada and abroad. The terminals have storage tanks and pipeline connections to refineries.

Safety and the environment

Small pipelines used for natural gas distribution can often be inserted underground with little surface disturbance. Larger pipelines – ranging from 100 millimetres to more than a metre in diameter – require careful planning before construction to make sure they can operate safely and reliably, with minimal risk of leaks or spills. After construction, the surface landscape is restored as nearly as possible to its previous state.

As with other industrial land use, pipeline projects require public consultation, landowner negotiations and environmental assessment. Prior to construction, pipeline companies survey proposed routes to determine soil characteristics, plant and animal types, archeological resources, and current land uses.

STAGES IN PIPELINE CONSTRUCTION

| 1. Land clearing | 2. Trenching | 3. Delivering pipe | 4. Welding |

©Canadian Centre for Energy Information 2009

The company works with stakeholders and government regulators to make sure routes are planned to minimize impacts on the land and populated areas. Several pipelines may run parallel on some routes. Laying them together in a single corridor reduces the effect on land use.

During construction or maintenance, layers of topsoil and subsoil are removed separately and later replaced over the pipeline. Companies choose methods to reduce impacts on plants and animals. Work may be rescheduled, for example, to avoid mating, nesting or migration seasons for wildlife species.

Following construction, the disturbed soil is usually revegetated using plants native to the surrounding environment. The land may also be returned to tilled agriculture or cattle grazing. In the event of a spill, contaminated soil may be moved to a landfill or cleaned by incineration or by a combination of evaporation and bacterial action.

Pipeline integrity

Design and construction decisions are guided by the comprehensive standards of CSA International (a division of the Canadian Standards Association), as well as by federal, provincial, territorial and, in some cases, municipal regulations. These standards and regulations set out design criteria and operating pressures, how deeply pipes are laid in the ground, and the thickness of pipe walls. Safety and integrity are also considered when selecting the material for the pipes and coatings. Different materials are used depending on the type of line and the products being transported. Although steel is most commonly used in the pipeline grid, distribution pipelines often use a type of plastic. All pipe is manufactured to strict CSA International standards and industry specifications. The outside of steel or aluminum pipelines is coated with a protective material before the pipe is laid in the ground. Technological advances in the chemistry and application of these coatings provide added protection against natural elements.

Larger diameter steel pipeline sections are typically welded together using an automated process that is monitored by experienced technicians. Throughout pipeline construction, non-destructive examinations (NDE) are carried out to ensure that pipe joints are welded to demanding specifications. These examinations include ultrasonics, which perform the same function as traditional radiography (a process similar to X-rays) but with additional features. Radiography provides information in two dimensions while ultrasonics offer a three-dimensional image of each weld. This greatly enhances the NDE operator's ability to identify imperfections in the welded joints of pipe so that they can be repaired immediately.

Pipelines are then pressure-tested for strength and integrity, usually by filling the pipe with water and compressing it to a pressure greater than the normal operating pressure. During construction, workers also install cathodic protection systems (low-voltage current) on the pipe to prevent electrochemical reactions that can cause steel to corrode.

Pipeline companies use sophisticated systems to avoid leaks and spills that might contaminate soil or fresh water supplies. The computerized control systems on pipelines are designed to detect pressure drops and quickly isolate sections of pipeline that might be leaking. Instrumentation devices called "smart pigs" are sent through pipelines regularly to conduct internal inspections. These devices detect corrosion or other defects that might lead to leaks or ruptures.

One common cause of accidents is damage from agricultural or construction activity near pipelines. Companies mark pipeline routes clearly and participate in various "call before you dig" programs to reduce this hazard. Aircraft are often used to patrol pipeline routes to look for this kind of activity and to detect natural hazards such as erosion. Monitoring on the ground augments aerial surveillance.

If an oil spill occurs, company crews and those from regional spill cleanup co-operatives are dispatched immediately to contain the oil and remove contamination. Vacuum trucks recover the majority of oil spilled on land, and it is sent for recycling. Cleanup techniques are similar to those used in the upstream petroleum industry.

Pipelines cross thousands of streams and rivers in Canada. During construction, the pipeline has traditionally been lowered into a trench excavated in the bottom of the waterway. New technologies use directional or horizontal drilling methods to bore under rivers. The pipe is then pulled through the borehole without any disturbance to the banks or the stream. This method has many potential applications. Construction schedules also avoid times when fish or waterfowl are vulnerable.

Offshore pipelines, such as those used for Sable Island natural gas off Nova Scotia, are buried in a trench on the bottom of the ocean.

Pipelines in Canada have recorded far fewer accidents and fatalities than other modes of transportation. According to the Transportation Safety Board of Canada, federally regulated pipelines reported 64 accidents in 2007, compared to 453 marine shipping accidents, 1,331 railway accidents and 284 aircraft accidents. There were no fatalities due to pipeline accidents in Canada between 1988 and 2008. By comparison, in 2007 alone there were 14 fatalities due to marine shipping accidents, 86 fatalities due to railway accidents and 49 fatalities due to aircraft accidents.

About half of all the pipelines in Canada are located in Alberta. The Alberta Energy Resources Conservation Board annual survey of provincially regulated pipeline performance in 2006

found there were 854 pipeline incidents in Alberta. Companies are required to report all spills, even very small ones, and all "hits" in which equipment contacts the pipeline. Only 18 of these were high-priority incidents that threatened serious environmental or public impact, and only 10 of all the incidents occurred on pipelines 40 centimetres in diameter or greater.

The ERCB report noted that over the previous decade the frequency of pipeline failures in the province dropped from five failures per 1,000 kilometres of pipeline to fewer than three. During 2006:

* 89.3 per cent of the pipeline incidents were leaks, 1.8 per cent were ruptures and 8.9 per cent were hits or incidents that did not result in a release
* The majority of failures occurred on small-diameter water lines and multiphase oil effluent lines that carry a mix of crude oil, water and natural gas
* There were more ruptures – 16 in 2006 compared to 13 in 2005
* 74 per cent were classified as "priority three", those having minimal potential for hazard or environmental impact.

The oil and gas industry invested $1.5 billion in pipeline integrity, maintenance and inspection during the preceding decade. The investment raised the standards for pipelines across the country.

In the mid-1990s, the National Energy Board launched an inquiry into a problem called "stress corrosion cracking" that had caused a number of pipeline failures. The board's report made 27 recommendations to promote public safety and pipeline integrity. The Canadian Energy Pipeline Association and the Canadian Association of Petroleum Producers subsequently developed manuals of

recommended practices to detect, repair and prevent pipeline failures due to stress corrosion cracking.

Aboriginal involvement

Establishing and maintaining good working relationships with Aboriginal people is a priority for pipeline companies whose operations can affect Aboriginal communities.

Pipeline companies encourage Aboriginal employment and the development of business opportunities for Aboriginal companies. Companies often achieve this goal by:

* reserving certain contracts for Aboriginal peoples
* breaking up larger contracts to give smaller contractors an opportunity to compete
* waiving bonding requirements where necessary
* requiring contractors to hire Aboriginals
* including an Aboriginal participation clause in all projects tendered, and
* establishing a management development program that provides qualified Aboriginal professionals with access to management positions within the industry.

Learn More

Developed by the Centre for Energy for the Canadian Energy Pipelines Association, Pipelines 101 addresses the growing need for balanced, factual information on Canada's pipelines and pipeline industry. Visit **www.cepa.com**

Photos courtesy of BJ Pipeline Inspection Services

Smart pigs

In-line inspection devices or "pigs" have been used for decades in the pipeline industry. They are propelled through the pipeline with the gas or liquid cargo to detect various kinds of defects. Pigs using sophisticated instrumentation such as magnetic field recorders or X-rays are known as "smart pigs." As technology has advanced, it has become possible to measure and record many characteristics of pipeline integrity.

Less sophisticated devices, known as "caliper pigs," test for gross deformities in the pipe by gauging variations in the internal diameter. Caliper pigs are sometimes used to ensure that a valuable smart pig will be able to pass through the line without being damaged or getting stuck.

Smart pigs such as the ones in these photos record the existence, location, and relative severity of the anomalies through use of recording equipment carried on board the pig. The pig is later recovered, and the data is downloaded for analysis by technicians and engineers. The analysis can often detect corrosion, cracks or small defects, and it provides guidance for companies in planning their maintenance programs. Any external anomalies can be examined visually to verify their existence and severity.

Smart pigs were initially used only on large-diameter transmission pipelines, but recent innovations have made it possible to use them to inspect relatively small pipelines, 20 centimetres or less in diameter. However, pigs may not be practical for pipelines that were not originally designed to accommodate them, including pipelines containing segments of different diameters, tight bends, restricted-bore valves, or pipelines with pressures or flow rates too low to propel the pig at the required speed. Pipelines built to carry natural gas tend to have tighter bends and more constrictions than those built to carry liquids.

Oil pipelines

Powerful electric motors drive the centrifugal pumps on most Canadian crude oil pipelines, although diesel engines are used in a few remote locations. Oil travels through the pipes at four to eight kilometres per hour, and it may take a month or more to carry crude oil to distant customers.

Unlike natural gas transmission pipelines, which primarily carry methane, liquids trunk lines may carry different types of crude oil, natural gas liquids and refined products. These different commodities travel through the pipe in batches that can be many kilometres long. Because every batch in a pipeline is traveling at the same speed, it is not necessary to separate them. Simple hydraulics prevent them from mixing except where they actually come in contact with each other, and these small volumes are reprocessed. Only rarely are metal or plastic "pigs" used to separate the batches. Complex networks of valves and storage tanks are used to make sure the batches get to the correct destinations. The batches move through the system like trains on railways.

The Guinness Book of World Records identifies the crude oil pipeline system of Enbridge Pipelines Inc. (formerly Interprovincial Pipe Line Inc.) as the world's longest petroleum pipeline system. It stretches from Norman Wells in the Northwest Territories to northern Alberta and from Edmonton eastward to Sarnia, Toronto, Montreal and the central United States. The leg between Sarnia and Montreal, originally built to carry Western Canadian crude oil eastward, was reversed in 1999 so that it now brings imported and offshore Canadian oil production westward to Ontario refineries.

MAJOR CRUDE OIL AND PRODUCTS PIPELINES

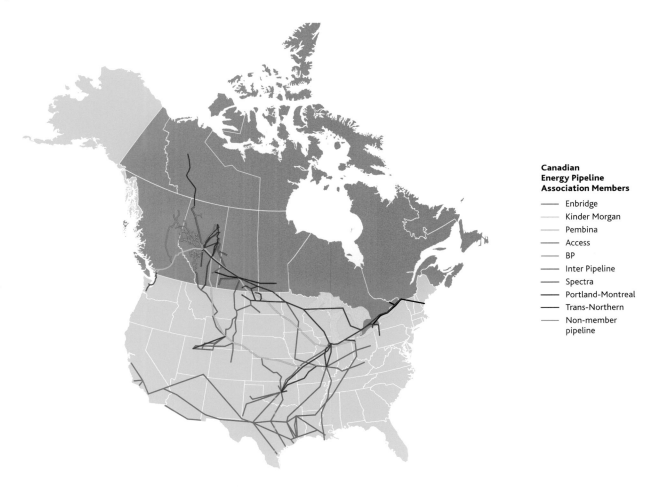

Canadian Energy Pipeline Association Members

- Enbridge
- Kinder Morgan
- Pembina
- Access
- BP
- Inter Pipeline
- Spectra
- Portland-Montreal
- Trans-Northern
- Non-member pipeline

©Canadian Centre for Energy Information 2009

The Trans Mountain system, owned by Kinder Morgan Canada Inc., carries crude oil and refined products westward from Edmonton to Vancouver and into Washington State. Kinder Morgan also operates the Express pipeline, which carries crude oil from Hardisty, Alberta, to Wyoming where it joins another Kinder Morgan pipeline, the Platte, to supply markets in the midwestern United States. Other pipelines that transport crude oil south from Alberta to Montana include the Rangeland, Milk River and Bow River systems. The Wascana pipeline carries crude oil from Saskatchewan into Montana.

Pipeline systems operated by Enbridge, Terasen and other companies also transport synthetic crude oil, heavy oil and bitumen to refineries and marketing terminals in Alberta. The Cochin pipeline carries natural gas liquids and petrochemicals from Alberta to Sarnia, and the Trans-Northern pipeline supplies refined petroleum products in southern Ontario and Quebec.

A network of gathering lines in the producing areas delivers crude oil to storage tanks along the main pipelines. If a well is not connected to a pipeline, the crude oil can be trucked to the nearest delivery point.

Canada's crude oil imports arrive by tankers at East Coast ports or at Portland, Maine, for shipment by pipeline to Montreal and to southern Ontario. There has also been some tanker transport of oil products on the Great Lakes.

CRUDE OIL PRODUCTION AND EQUIVALENT SUPPLY AND DISTRIBUTION
(Mbbl/d)

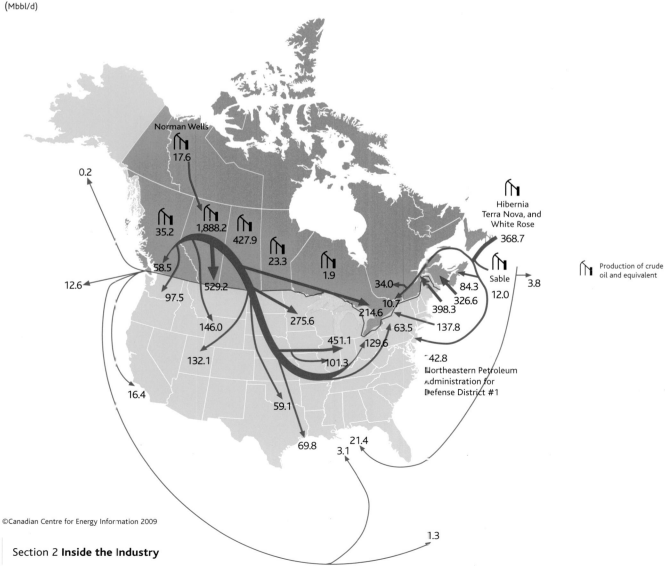

©Canadian Centre for Energy Information 2009

Natural gas pipelines

Gas turbines – similar to the engines of jet airliners, but burning natural gas as fuel – spin the centrifugal pumps that compress natural gas in major transmission lines. Compressed up to 100 times the pressure of the atmosphere, the gas moves up to 40 kilometres per hour, travelling from Alberta to southern Ontario in about six days.

The Alberta Gas Transmission division of TransCanada PipeLines Limited (TCPL) carries the greatest volume of natural gas in Canada. The Alberta system carries gas from producing areas around the province to distribution systems, industrial customers and other transmission systems serving markets in Canada and the United States.

TCPL also owns the main interprovincial natural gas pipeline in Canada. It is one of the world's longest natural gas transmission lines, extending from the eastern Alberta border into Quebec with numerous connections to the United States.

In British Columbia, Spectra Energy operates gathering lines and gas processing plants as well as the main natural gas transmission system.

TransGas Limited operates the collection system in Saskatchewan.

The Maritimes & Northeast Pipeline main pipeline was built in 1999 to bring natural gas to markets in the Maritimes and Northeastern United States from six developed natural gas fields 160 kilometres offshore Nova Scotia. The natural gas is delivered to shore by a pipeline laid in a trench on the sea floor. The Canadian portion of the onshore main line stretches 568 kilometres from Goldboro, Nova Scotia to St. Stephen, New Brunswick.

MAJOR NATURAL GAS TRANSMISSION LINES

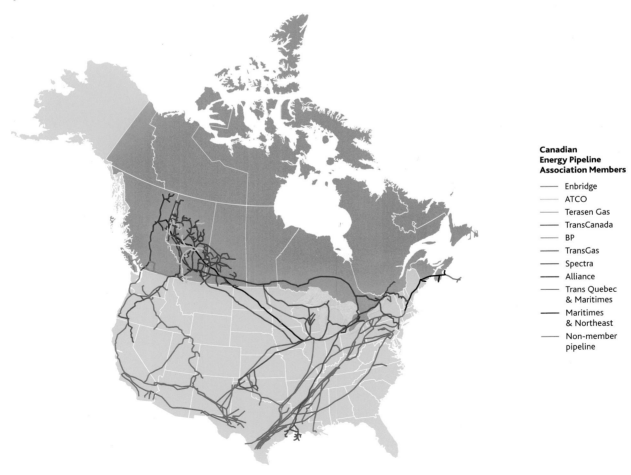

Canadian Energy Pipeline Association Members

- Enbridge
- ATCO
- Terasen Gas
- TransCanada
- BP
- TransGas
- Spectra
- Alliance
- Trans Quebec & Maritimes
- Maritimes & Northeast
- Non-member pipeline

©Canadian Centre for Energy Information 2009

The Alliance Pipeline, which began operation in late 2000, stretches from northeastern British Columbia to the Chicago area, and carries both natural gas and natural gas liquids. Other significant transmission systems include Trans Quebec & Maritimes Pipeline Inc. in Quebec and Terasen Gas, which operates a natural gas pipeline to Vancouver Island.

Local distribution companies deliver natural gas to consumers in each of the gas-consuming provinces. New natural gas distribution systems are being developed in Nova Scotia and New Brunswick as gas becomes available from the area near Sable Island.

To balance supply and demand, several natural gas companies operate storage facilities in depleted oil and gas fields and underground salt caverns. The largest facilities are located in central and eastern Alberta and southwestern Ontario.

Selling crude oil and natural gas

Crude oil and natural gas are sold by the supply or marketing departments of production companies, by groups of producers, and by independent marketers. The buyers include oil refineries, petrochemical companies, industrial and commercial customers, electric power producers and local gas distribution companies. In some cases, even individual customers such as schools and hospitals

can buy directly from producers or marketers. The field price is the amount received by producers after deducting transportation and marketing costs.

Did you know?

Natural gas moves through pipelines up to 40 kilometres per hour, about the speed of an Olympic sprinter. Crude oil averages about five kilometres per hour through pipelines, roughly walking speed.

NATURAL GAS PRODUCTION AND DISTRIBUTION (Bcf/d)

Natural gas production

Major export points:

Ⓐ Huntingdon
Ⓑ Kingsgate
Ⓒ Monchy
Ⓓ Elmore
Ⓔ Emerson
Ⓕ Niagara Falls
Ⓖ Iroquois
Ⓗ St. Stephen

©Canadian Centre for Energy Information 2009

Crude oil benchmarks

The key market for establishing Canadian crude oil prices is the Chicago area, where western Canadian oil competes with U.S. and foreign supplies. The most widely quoted North American crude type is West Texas Intermediate (WTI). Due to daily futures trading on financial markets such as the New York Mercantile Exchange, WTI has become one of the world's benchmark crudes for determining the prices of specific grades of oil at various locations. Its price reflects worldwide oil supply and demand as well as the conditions in the North American market.

The price of North Sea Brent crude is another benchmark used in international crude oil marketing. In Canada, domestic crude oil prices such as the Edmonton par price are largely determined by the price of competing crude oils in the Chicago market.

A competitive international market

Transportation costs are the main reason why crude oil prices vary from place to place. If the price offered by buyers in one market is too low, then sellers will ship their oil to another market – if they can afford the

transportation cost and there is available transportation capacity.

While the major factor determining Canadian crude oil pricing is the price of benchmark crudes such as WTI, prices are also influenced by the availability of pipeline shipping capacity and the supply and demand for specific grades of light or heavy crude oil, with high or low sulphur content.

Price differentials

Refining light crude oil typically produces a higher proportion of desirable products such as gasoline and diesel fuel, compared with the products

INTERNATIONAL CRUDE OIL PRICING

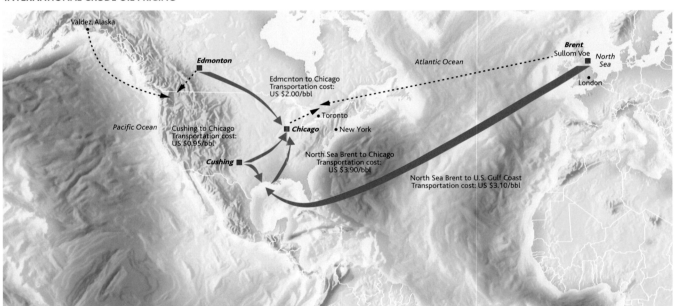

CRUDE OIL PRICES AND TRANSPORTATION COSTS

Edmonton par

2008 Price (U.S. $/bbl)	98.72
2007 Transport costs Edmonton - Chicago	$ 2.00

The Edmonton par price is the amount offered by Edmonton refineries for light sweet crude oil (40 on the American Petroleum Institute gravity scale with 0.5 per cent sulphur content). The average Edmonton par price posted by Imperial Oil, Petro-Canada, Shell and Suncor for May 2009 and adjusted to 0.5 per cent sulphur content was Cdn $64.31 per 159-litre barrel, equivalent to U.S. $55.88 per barrel.

West Texas Intermediate

2008 Price (U.S. $/bbl)	100.25
2007 Transport Costs Cushing - Chicago	$ 0.95

West Texas Intermediate (WTI) is a light grade of U.S. crude oil (40 on the American Petroleum Institute gravity scale, with 0.5 per cent sulphur content) widely traded on commodity markets. The price is established for deliveries of this crude to a terminal at Cushing, Oklahoma.

North Sea Brent

2008 Price (U.S. $/bbl)	98.93
2007 Transport Costs North Sea - Chicago	$ 3.90
2007 Transport Costs North Sea - Gulf Coast	$ 3.10

North Sea Brent is another crude oil commonly traded on international commodity markets. The price refers to a grade of crude oil (37 on the American Petroleum Institute gravity scale, with one per cent sulphur content) which is somewhat heavier and more sour than Edmonton par or WTI. The Brent price is quoted for deliveries to the Sullom Voe terminal in the North Sea.

◀ Major crude oil transportation route

◀- - - Other key markets affecting Canadian crude oil prices

The ocean-going oil tanker is the cheapest form of long-distance energy transportation, while the crude oil pipeline is the second cheapest. The relatively low cost of moving crude oil between regions and continents explains why oil prices are similar around the world.

Source: Canadian Association of Petroleum Producers

derived from refining heavy oil. To produce the same proportion of desirable products, heavy oil requires additional refining processes. Heavier crude oil therefore sells for less.

In addition, pipeline tariffs for heavy oils are higher because more energy is required to move them through the pipeline, and because they move more slowly through the pipeline system, restricting the amount of crude oil that can be shipped. The price also depends on the sulphur content; high-sulphur sour crude sells for a lower price than sweet crude because more processing is required.

Natural gas pricing

Pricing of natural gas is very competitive and fluctuates according to many factors. The current and expected balance of supply and demand within North America is a primary consideration. Within a geographic region, the price may be depressed if there is insufficient pipeline capacity to deliver available natural gas to other markets. This situation existed in Western Canada in the late 1990s before the Alliance Pipeline was built from Western Canada to central U.S. markets.

Some natural gas is shipped internationally as liquefied natural gas (LNG) carried in special tankers. Thus far, LNG shipments have had little impact on North American natural gas prices. Nine LNG receiving terminals have been proposed in Canada, two in British Columbia and seven on the East Coast. The first of these, Canaport in Saint John, New Brunswick is due to start operations in 2009. Volumes received by the eight U.S. terminals (four on the East Coast, four on the Gulf of Mexico) provided about 1.5 per cent of U.S. natural gas consumption in 2008.

Additional factors include the costs of natural gas transportation, storage and distribution and prices of competing

energy supplies such as crude oil, coal, nuclear power and hydroelectricity.

Residential natural gas customers served by local distribution companies use the gas mostly for home heating during winter months. By contrast, large industrial customers generally consume natural gas throughout the year. Some large industrial customers that are able to use alternate fuels such as heavy fuel oil may sign "interruptible" natural gas contracts in order to negotiate lower prices for natural gas. Those customers would have their natural gas supply shut off during infrequent periods of very high natural gas demand, which usually occurs during extremely cold weather. The cost of serving industrial customers is often less than that of residential customers because of the larger volume consumed and the nature of the interruptible service.

Natural gas distribution

Natural gas is delivered to Canadian consumers by provincially regulated utilities called local distribution companies. These companies generally buy natural gas from producers or marketers and then resell it to their

customers. However, some consumers can buy natural gas directly from suppliers and just pay distribution companies for the delivery service they provide.

Local distribution companies operate more than 237,000 kilometres of pipelines in Canada. Rural Alberta gas co-operatives operate another 66,000 kilometres. These pipelines range from high-pressure main distribution lines up to 61 centimetres in diameter to low-pressure, 2.5-centimetre steel or plastic tubing used in residential service lines.

Efficiency and emissions

Distribution companies are working with customers to improve the efficiency of natural gas use. Educational campaigns and energy audits identify opportunities for efficiency gains. For example, the typical home furnace installed in the 1970s utilized about 65 per cent of the heating value of natural gas, while modern furnaces capture up to 95 per cent of the heat.

According to the Canadian Gas Association, greenhouse gas emissions from local distribution companies are

NATURAL GAS LOCAL DISTRIBUTION SYSTEM

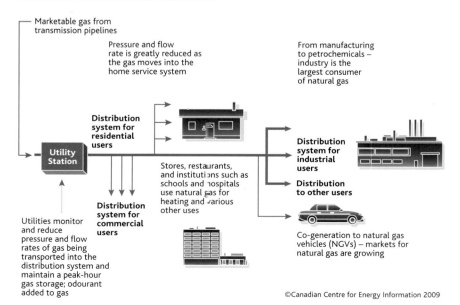

Marketable gas from transmission pipelines

Pressure and flow rate is greatly reduced as the gas moves into the home service system

From manufacturing to petrochemicals – industry is the largest consumer of natural gas

Distribution system for residential users

Utility Station

Utilities monitor and reduce pressure and flow rates of gas being transported into the distribution system and maintain a peak-hour gas storage; odourant added to gas

Distribution system for commercial users

Stores, restaurants, and institutions such as schools and hospitals use natural gas for heating and various other uses

Distribution system for industrial users

Distribution to other users

Co-generation to natural gas vehicles (NGVs) – markets for natural gas are growing

©Canadian Centre for Energy Information 2009

about 0.5 per cent of total human-caused greenhouse gas emissions in Canada. From 2000 to 2004, emissions from natural gas distribution operations were reduced by 6 per cent.

Pipelines accounted for about 1.3 per cent of Canada's human-caused greenhouse gas emissions in 2006 although they carried more than two-thirds of Canada's primary energy supply. This is down from 1.8 per cent in 1995.

An analysis by the Canadian Gas Association estimated 75 per cent of the greenhouse gas emissions from natural gas in Canada in 2000 occurred at the point of end use, while 14.3 per cent occurred in productions and processing, 9.9 per cent in transmission and storage, and 0.8 per cent in distribution. However, a significant portion of the industry's emissions results from the export of approximately half of Canada's natural gas production to the United States. Other studies indicate that up to 84 per cent of the greenhouse gas emissions from natural gas occur at the point of final combustion.

Natural gas is sometimes called a "clean energy" fuel because the main products of combustion are water vapour and carbon dioxide. The emissions of carbon dioxide from natural gas are up to 50 per cent less than those derived from an energy-equivalent amount of refined oil products.

The greenhouse gas emissions are less because the methane in natural gas contains four hydrogen atoms for every carbon atom. When natural gas burns, a lot of the energy comes from burning this hydrogen, which forms water vapour. By contrast, diesel fuel and heating oil contain approximately two hydrogen atoms for every carbon atom, so twice as much carbon must be burned to produce the same amount of energy as from an equivalent amount of natural gas. Burning more carbon produces more carbon dioxide.

In general, the natural gas industry contributes to Canada's climate change and air quality objectives by encouraging the efficient use of gas, managing direct emissions, facilitating end use energy efficiency and promoting the development of energy efficient end use technologies.

Co-generation – an example of complex issues

The fastest-growing use of natural gas since the early 1990s has been for the generation of electricity. Many industrial companies and utilities across Canada have installed gas-fired generation and co-generation facilities. In co-generation, gas is burned usually in a turbine, to power electrical generators. The "waste heat" from the turbine is used to produce steam to provide heat for buildings and industrial processes.

Natural gas co-generation is highly energy-efficient and emits fewer pollutants than any other non-nuclear thermal-electric system. Efficiency is determined by comparing the total energy (kilowatts or gigajoules) going into a facility with the amounts of useful energy such as steam or electricity that it produces. Natural gas co-generation is about 65 to 80 per cent energy-efficient compared to about 40 per cent energy efficiency for the best conventional coal-fired electric power plants. Sulphur dioxide and mercury emissions from natural gas-fired co-generation are virtually zero, while emissions of carbon dioxide and nitrogen oxides are considerably lower than from coal or oil. In some instances, emissions from coal- or oil-fired generators are also reduced by using some natural gas either as part of the fuel or to re-burn the main burner emissions.

However, raw natural gas must first be processed in order to provide the clean-burning fuel that these co-generation facilities require. Processing natural gas causes emissions of sulphur dioxide and carbon dioxide in gas producing areas. In other words, an environmental benefit for one region may involve an environmental cost for another. Future attempts to include environmental values in the economic system must address these and other complex issues.

Natural gas for vehicles

In Canada, about 38,000 motor vehicles, mainly in British Columbia and Ontario, have been adapted to operate on natural gas. The advantages of natural gas vehicles (NGVs) include reduced emissions of greenhouse gases and other pollutants. Disadvantages include the cost of converting vehicles, the cost of compressors for fuelling, the space needed in vehicles for gas cylinders, the weight of the cylinders, the number of refuelling stations and the relatively short driving distance between refuellings. NGV use has been encouraged by availability of government subsidies for conversion and tax relief on the fuel price.

About 180,000 vehicles have also been converted to run on propane, a natural gas liquid extracted from natural gas.

Onward to the consumer

Natural gas and propane are about the only petroleum commodities that can be used by the end consumer in almost the same form they leave the upstream producing area. Even for these two fuels, a smelly substance called mercaptan is usually added to the naturally odourless gases as a safety warning before they are sent on to the end user. Mercaptan gives the gas a strong, pungent smell to help to detect leaks. However, the majority of petroleum hydrocarbons require further processing and manufacturing.

The next chapter describes how the molecules are mixed, sorted and formulated into marketable products.

Photo courtesy of Shell Canada

The challenge

The refining and petrochemicals sector applies chemistry and physics to make products desired by consumers and industry. The challenge is to do this cost-efficiently, with the fewest possible effects on health, safety and the environment.

Refining, petroleum products and petrochemicals – manufacturing molecules

Petroleum molecules come in a wide variety of sizes and shapes – strings and rings of carbon and hydrogen atoms. The methane in natural gas is the simplest and smallest. By comparison, the molecules in lubricants, heavy fuel oil and asphalt are large and complex.

These hydrocarbon molecules are sorted, split apart, reassembled and blended at refineries and petrochemical plants. There, they become part of a multitude of products, from gasoline to synthetic rubber. This is accomplished by physical separations and chemical reactions. Temperature, pressure and catalysts play a dominant role. Catalysts are materials that assist chemical reactions.

During the past 30 years, the refining and petrochemical sectors have led Canadian industries in the application of state-of-the-art computer technology and process controls. These technologies have helped companies improve efficiency and product quality while reducing air and water pollution.

Oil refineries

An oil refinery is a manufacturing facility that uses crude oil as a raw material and produces a mix of products. The mix can be varied to a limited extent by changing the types of processing units or the process conditions or by using different crude oil feedstocks. In summer, for example, Canadian refineries increase their output of gasoline for motorists and their production of asphalt for road paving. In winter, they refine more home heating and diesel fuels.

All refineries are different. Some can process heavy crude oils or synthetic crudes, while others only process conventional light sweet crude oil. The degree of flexibility is a key factor in refinery competitiveness.

The downstream oil products industry

Canadian refining and petrochemical plants, from coast to coast, employed more than 20,000 people in 2003. Ten companies operate 16 oil refineries that produce gasoline and other products such as diesel, jet fuel, heating oil and kerosene. These operations directly employed about 6,200 Canadians in 2006. Approximately 101,500 people were employed in wholesaling, marketing, distributing and retailing refined oil products.

During the 1980s, consumption of refined petroleum products in Canada declined about 20 per cent to a total of about 80 billion litres per year. Consumption dropped because of more efficient vehicles, slower economic growth, and a shift from oil products to natural gas for heating and some industrial processes. In the 1990s, use of petroleum products began increasing again due to population growth, economic recovery, and the popularity of light trucks, vans and sport utility vehicles. Almost all of the increased demand was for transportation fuels. In 2008, consumption totalled 103 billion litres – including about 42 billion litres of motor gasoline and 28 billion litres of diesel fuel.

The heart of the refining process

As a raw product, crude oil is of limited use. Refineries must separate and process the mix of hydrocarbons that make up crude oil before they can be transformed into hundreds of useful products such as gasoline, diesel and jet fuel.

The first and most critical step in processing crude oil is to separate it into various components or fractions. This occurs in a fractionating column, also known as an atmospheric distillation tower – a tall steel tower layered with perforated trays. Since each fraction has a different boiling range, a distillation tower is able to separate the various fractions using heat and cooling.

CANADIAN OIL REFINERIES

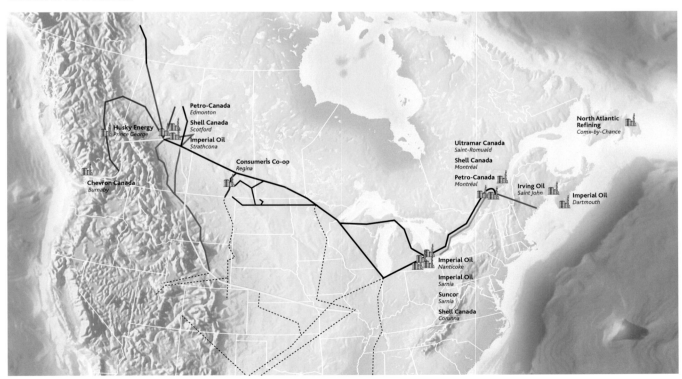

Petro-Canada *Edmonton*

Shell Canada *Scotford*

Husky Energy *Prince George*

Imperial Oil *Strathcona*

Consumer's Co-op *Regina*

Chevron Canada *Burnaby*

Ultramar Canada *Saint-Romuald*

Shell Canada *Montréal*

Petro-Canada *Montréal*

Irving Oil *Saint John*

Imperial Oil *Dartmouth*

North Atlantic Refining *Come-by-Chance*

Imperial Oil *Nanticoke*

Imperial Oil *Sarnia*

Suncor *Sarnia*

Shell Canada *Corunna*

©Canadian Centre for Energy Information 2009

Atmospheric distillation

1 Gases and light gasoline. The gases (methane, ethane, propane, and butane) are commonly used to fuel refinery furnaces while the light gasoline is routed to gasoline blending.

2 Light distillates (naphtha, kerosene). Naphtha is used in the production of gasoline and petrochemicals. Kerosene was originally used as a lamp oil; today it is primarily used as a jet fuel and stove oil.

3 Middle distillates (light and heavy gas oils). Light gas oils are made into jet, diesel and furnace fuels. Heavy gas oils undergo further chemical processing such as cracking to produce naphtha and other products.

4 Residual products are further processed to produce refinery fuels, heavy fuel oil (bunker oil), waxes, greases and asphalt.

DETAIL OF PERFORATING TRAY

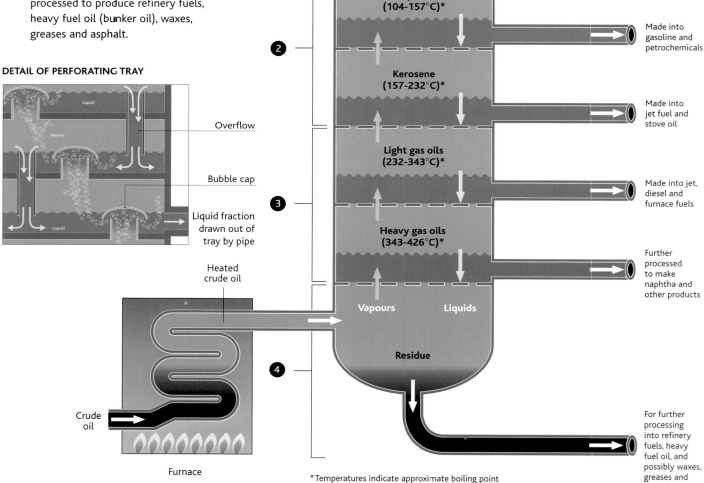

SIMPLIFIED CROSS-SECTION OF DISTILLATION TOWER

Liquid

Vapour

Liquid

Overflow

Bubble cap

Liquid fraction drawn out of tray by pipe

Heated crude oil

Crude oil

Furnace

Rising vapours

Naphtha (104-157°C)*

Kerosene (157-232°C)*

Light gas oils (232-343°C)*

Heavy gas oils (343-426°C)*

Vapours   Liquids

Residue

Gases (up to 32°C)* Fuel refinery furnaces

Light gasoline (32-104°C)* Routed to blending

Made into gasoline and petrochemicals

Made into jet fuel and stove oil

Made into jet, diesel and furnace fuels

Further processed to make naphtha and other products

For further processing into refinery fuels, heavy fuel oil, and possibly waxes, greases and asphalt

*Temperatures indicate approximate boiling point of each hydrocarbon fraction

©Canadian Centre for Energy Information 2009

Heavier hydrocarbons boil at much higher temperatures than their lighter counterparts. They tend to settle in trays at the bottom of the tower closest to the furnace, while lighter fractions tend to collect at the top.

Distillation is a continuous process that begins by heating crude oil in a furnace until it turns into a vapour. The vapour rises through perforations in the trays that are fitted with bubble caps. These caps force the vapour to bubble through a previously liquefied fraction in the tray.

Bubbling cools the vapour enough for it to shed the heaviest fraction, which condenses onto the tray. The remaining vapour repeats this process as it continues upward; as each fraction reaches the tray where the temperature is just below its own boiling point, it condenses, liquefies and is drawn off the tray by pipes. A number of trays are needed to collect the liquids from each fraction.

Other refining processes

Following distillation, many of the separated streams undergo further chemical processing or purification before they can be blended into marketable commodities.

If the refinery operator aims to get a higher yield of transportation fuels, the heavier fractions recovered from distillation undergo cracking processes similar to those employed in the upgrading of heavy oil and bitumen (described on page 82 and 83). Cracking breaks large molecules into smaller ones. This is done by various combinations of heat, pressure and catalysts. Most processes either add hydrogen (hydrotreating or hydrocracking) or remove carbon (coking) during the process.

Other refining processes rearrange or rebuild the hydrocarbon molecules.

These processes include:

- *Alkylation* uses an acid catalyst to combine light molecules, such as propylene and butylene, with isobutane; this produces larger, branched-chain molecules (isoparaffins) called alkylate, a valuable, high-octane gasoline blending component.

- *Isomerization* is a chemical process that rearranges straight-chain hydrocarbons (paraffins) into branched-chain hydrocarbons called isoparaffins (isomerate, another high-octane gasoline blending component). Isomerization is used to produce isobutane for alkylation and to convert pentanes and hexanes into higher-octane compounds (isomers) for use in blending gasoline.

- *Catalytic* reforming uses catalysts to upgrade naphtha into high-octane gasoline and petrochemical feedstocks such as benzene and toluene. Naphthas are low-boiling-point hydrocarbon mixtures containing many paraffins (chain molecules) and some naphthenes (ring molecules).

Products from refining

About three-quarters of the volume of crude oil processed at Canadian refineries is converted into transportation fuels – gasoline, diesel fuel, aviation jet fuel and fuel oil for locomotives and ships. Increased demand for transportation fuels has been offset in the past quarter-century by a decrease in the use of heating oil, which has been replaced in many areas by natural gas. The other products obtained from crude oil refining include asphalt, lubricants, waxes, the raw materials for petrochemicals and fuel oil burned to generate electricity. The refining process itself consumes about five per cent of the crude oil, or

an equivalent amount of energy from other sources such as natural gas.

Fuel formulation

New engine designs and environmental regulations have required many changes in the way transportation fuels are refined and blended. One big change was the elimination of lead from gasoline between 1973 and 1990. Recent measures have reduced the benzene content of gasoline and are greatly reducing the sulphur content of both gasoline and diesel fuel.

New ways of boosting octane, a measure of the speed and evenness of combustion, are still being explored. In general, there are two ways to match the octane of unleaded gasoline to the needs of engines: more intense refining at a higher cost or reformulating the gasoline with various additives or blend stocks. For example, gasoline can be altered by adding high-octane ethanol (ethyl alcohol). Refiners assess product marketability and the impact on both vehicles and the environment as they seek the most cost-effective solutions.

There are both technological and economic challenges in reformulating fuels to meet ever-more-stringent environmental requirements as well as new engine designs and consumers' performance expectations. So far, there do not appear to be any perfect solutions. For example, ethanol reduces hydrocarbon and carbon monoxide emissions, but it has a lower energy content per litre, and may increase emissions of nitrogen oxides and other substances.

Addressing the smog issue

Ground-level ozone, the major component of smog, is a concern in some regions. It is formed when volatile organic compounds (VOCs) and nitrogen oxides react in the presence of sunlight. VOCs are released into the atmosphere when tank trucks load and unload, when consumers put fuel in their vehicles, and from vehicle fuel tanks and exhaust tailpipes. VOCs are also produced naturally from vegetation and from forest fires.

The petroleum industry is participating in programs to reduce VOC emissions. Recovery systems recycle the vapours normally displaced into the atmosphere during truck loading and delivery by directing the vapours back into the truck tank or storage tank. Vapour recovery equipment installed at industry bulk transfer facilities in southern Ontario and the B.C. Lower Mainland has helped to reduce smog in these areas.

Beginning with the 1998 model year, all vehicles sold in Canada have been equipped with large onboard canisters containing absorbent carbon to capture and recycle vapour during refueling.

In addition, refiners reduce the volatility of gasolines produced in summer months across Canada, which reduces vapour emissions during the critical period for smog formation. However, volatility cannot be reduced too much because this would cause start-up and driveability problems for some vehicles.

Benzene and sulphur

One of the VOCs is benzene, which has been identified as a potential cancer-causing compound. Benzene occurs naturally in petroleum and is also produced by some refining processes and by combustion of fuels in engines.

By 2002, refinery emissions of benzene were reduced by 86 per cent from 1993 levels, and the benzene content of gasoline had been cut by more than 50 per cent. In 1999, legislation took effect

AVERAGE BENZENE CONTENT OF CANADIAN GASOLINE
(volume per cent)

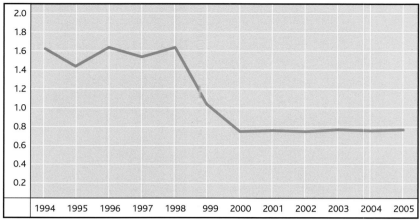

Source: Environment Canada

REDUCING BENZENE EMISSIONS
Reductions in the benzene content of gasoline, combined with improvements in vehicle emission controls and vapour recovery at retail outlets, led to a significant reduction in benzene concentrations in urban areas in Canada.

VOLUME WEIGHTED SULPHUR LEVELS IN MOTOR GASOLINE
(miligrams per kilogram)

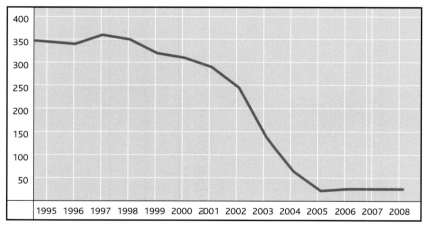

Source: Environment Canada

REDUCING SULPHUR
Until July 1 2002, the regulated limit of sulphur in gasoline was 1,000 mg/kg. From July 1, 2002 to December 31, 2004, the regulated limit was 150 mg/kg. Since January 1, 2005 the regulated limit has been 30 mg/kg.

limiting the benzene content of gasoline to no more than one per cent. Current exposure levels of workers are well within provincial health standards.

Another issue has been the sulphur content of gasoline and the emission of sulphur compounds and particulates from diesel engines. These emissions are a public health concern and also contribute to smog. Federal regulations enacted in 2001 cut the maximum sulphur by over 95 per cent in gasoline in 2005, and in diesel fuel in 2006. To meet these requirements, refiners

invested five billion dollars to reduce sulphur levels in both gasoline and diesel fuel.

Refineries and the environment

Refineries improved the energy efficiency of their processes by 30 per cent between 1970 and 1990, and a further 20 per cent between 1990 and 2005. Greater energy efficiency brought a comparable reduction in refineries' greenhouse gas emissions.

New technologies also brought substantial reductions in emissions of sulphur dioxide, carbon monoxide, nitrogen oxides, hydrocarbons and particulates. Refineries have installed new waste treatment systems, odour scrubbers, noise suppressants and water purification facilities. These modifications are the result of industry initiatives that addressed occupational health and safety requirements, community concerns, municipal bylaws and provincial regulations.

In Ontario, for example, refiners spent $350 million over two decades to eliminate 99 per cent of the trace contaminants in their waste water. They led all industrial sectors in setting new standards for compliance with environmental regulations.

Refineries use large volumes of water for heating, cooling and cleaning processes. Recycling and water conservation measures have substantially reduced this water use. Improved wastewater treatment makes sure that releases meet federal water quality standards. According to the Canadian Petroleum Products Institute, from 1993 to 2005, atmospheric emissions of nine of the ten most common substances declined by amounts ranging from 76 per cent to 86 per cent. Of these emissions, the three main substances involved are xylenes, toluene and propylene.

Petroleum products manufacturers provide spill containment equipment and training to avoid spills that might contaminate water supplies. Companies work with government environmental protection officials to prevent contaminants from reaching water resources when spills occur.

The Canadian Council of Ministers of the Environment developed an approach to reduce emissions from the petroleum-refining sector. This initiative is intended to lead to better air quality and help reduce negative health impacts such as respiratory and chronic illnesses that are caused by air contaminants.

Called the National Framework for Petroleum Refinery Emission Reductions (NFPRER) it was first proposed in 2001 by the Canadian Petroleum Products Institute, and includes all levels of government, industry, and non-governmental environmental and health organizations working together. The NFPRER provides the principles and methods for various jurisdictions to establish facility emissions caps for key air pollutants and air toxics from petroleum refineries.

Petrochemical plants

Petrochemicals are manufactured from natural gas (methane), natural gas liquids (ethane, propane, butane and condensates) and from by-products of oil refining such as naphtha. Ethane, for example, is used as a feedstock to produce ethylene, which in turn is used to manufacture polyethylene for cord, rope and flexible packaging material, and styrene, which is used for expanded polystyrene cups and many other consumer products. Nylon and detergents are other examples of materials made from petrochemicals.

Petrochemical plants produce single chemicals, or a small number of chemical compounds, for subsequent processing into finished products by other industries. The major petrochemical building blocks produced in Canada are methanol, ethylene, propylene, styrene, butadiene, butylene, benzene, toluene and xylene. These compounds are then further manufactured into products as varied as synthetic rubber, plastic bags, polyvinyl chloride (PVC) pipe, antifreeze, insulation and pesticides.

Propane is often used as both a feedstock and a fuel for petrochemical plants. Products manufactured from propane include both car antifreeze and the plastic container in which it is sold. Other products include polyester clothing, plastic auto parts and children's toys, plastic pipes and hoses, polypropylene rope, synthetic carpets, soap and the solvents used by dry cleaners.

The Canadian Chemical Producers Association (CCPA) estimates that about 83,000 Canadians are employed in the chemical industry. The "business of chemistry" – including petrochemicals – is worth $17 billion annually in Canada, and its products are used in final manufacturing of products worth $35 billion annually. The petrochemical business is cyclical, which means that prices and growth vary over time according to changes in production capacity and global economic activity.

The CCPA, representing major petrochemical companies, has adopted a comprehensive code of practice called Responsible Care®. The initiative emphasizes accountability, dialogue, teamwork and continuous improvement in the development of environmental policies. Companies work in partnership with contractors, suppliers and customers to ensure a life-cycle approach to chemicals management. This means that the industry considers factors such as reuse, recycling and disposal as well as production and marketing.

Did you know?

Gasoline accounts for about 40 per cent of the crude oil volume processed by Canadian refineries.

The challenge

Marketing people face intense competition for the consumer dollar, and must also maintain high standards of protection for health, safety and the environment.

Marketing – fuels for Canadians

Transportation fuels – gasoline, diesel fuel, jet fuel and marine fuel oil – are critical products of crude oil refining. They are the largest source of oil industry revenues, and they are vital to the North American economy.

The retailer is usually the only direct connection between the petroleum industry and the consumer. Retail outlets often sell diesel fuel and propane, and sometimes natural gas for vehicles, as well as gasoline and lubricants. Other petroleum retailers include: bulk stations, cardlock facilities for truck fleets, fuel oil and propane dealers, aviation and marine fuel dealers, and natural gas distribution companies. Home heating fuel dealers, docks and marinas are significant points of contact between the industry and its customers. Other dealers distribute to bulk customers in industries such as farming, forestry and mining.

The marketing sector of the oil and gas industry has many functions beyond retailing. Marketing companies purchase fuels from other suppliers as well as their own refineries, and then must store, blend and deliver fuels to meet their dealers' and customers' needs. Experts manage the health, safety and environmental aspects of fuel handling. Sales representatives work with fleet operators to meet their special needs, and deal with specialized markets such as fishing, forestry and mining. Lubricants, antifreeze and other products must be developed, packaged and marketed. In recent years, non-fuel goods and services – convenience stores, food outlets and car washes, for example – have become a big part of retail gasoline marketing in Canada. The economics of marketing continue to evolve and become ever more complex.

Gasoline pricing

Retailers must find a balance between a price that is high enough to cover all their business operating costs yet is low enough to attract customers. Prices move in reaction to local competition. Consumers choose the station that offers the best combination of price, convenience and service.

Prices vary considerably from day to day and city to city for a variety of reasons. Competition among stations is the dominant reason for local price changes. Other factors include supply and demand, taxation, cost of crude oil, wholesale price and average sales volumes. Numerous government studies of gasoline pricing over the past 25 years have concluded that the retail market in Canada is highly competitive.

The downstream environment

Throughout the oil and gas industry, underground storage tanks have been removed or upgraded to prevent leakage that might contaminate soil and ground water.

When retail outlets, refineries and other downstream facilities are closed, sites are tested for possible contamination. The procedures for cleaning up contaminated sites are similar to those used in the upstream petroleum industry. Cleanup continues until the site meets the standards established for commercial, industrial, residential or recreational uses, as appropriate. Cleaning up a single site when a retail outlet is closed can easily cost $500,000, and many sites cost more than $1 million to remediate.

CANADIAN AVERAGE GASOLINE PRICE COMPONENTS (Based on $1.00 per litre)

- ■ Taxes
- ■ Crude oil costs
- ■ Refining operating margin
- ■ Marketing operating margin

Source: Canadian Association of Petroleum Producers

Where does your gasoline dollar go?

According to a survey of retail prices in 10 cities in May 2009, federal and provincial taxes accounted for 33 per cent of the average price of a litre of gasoline. The cost of crude oil accounted for 42 per cent of the average consumer price in this period. The remaining 25 per cent went to cover refining and marketing costs, including the station's operating costs and margins.

INTERNATIONAL RETAIL GASOLINE PRICES ($ Cdn per litre) *2008 Average Price*

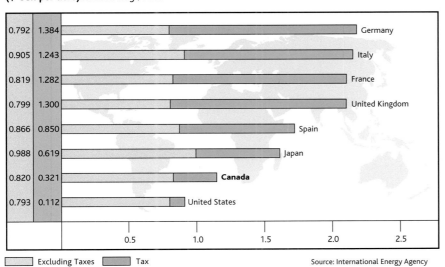

	Excluding Taxes				Tax	

0.792	1.384	Germany
0.905	1.243	Italy
0.819	1.282	France
0.799	1.300	United Kingdom
0.866	0.850	Spain
0.988	0.619	Japan
0.820	0.321	**Canada**
0.793	0.112	United States

0.5   1.0   1.5   2.0   2.5

☐ Excluding Taxes   ☐ Tax   Source: International Energy Agency

Used oil – a challenge for the industry

The Canadian Petroleum Products Institute (CPPI) estimates that Canadians improperly dispose of more than 150 million litres of used motor oil every year. Most of this comes from do-it-yourself home oil changers. Just one litre of used oil can contaminate one million litres of fresh water.

CPPI members, other producers and retailers, with the support of provincial and federal governments, have implemented a program to recover and properly dispose of the used oil.

This national plan focuses on the do-it-yourself oil changer and emphasizes that all sellers must participate in efforts to collect used oil. The used oil can be re-refined or reprocessed for reuse.

Alternately, used oil can be used as fuel in cement kilns or in industrial and utility boilers equipped with appropriate pollution controls.

87 million litres re-refined by CCPI member
7.3%

654.5 million litres consumed
55%

135.5 million litres inproperly disposed of
11.4%

313 million litres re-refined/reused by other
26.3%

Did you know?

Between 1998 and 2008, the number of retail service stations in Canada declined almost 17.5 per cent, from 15,380 to 12,684. About half sell under the brand names of major refining companies. Independent owners, regional companies and retail chains operate the remainder.

Getting the most value from your gasoline dollar

Consumers can get more value from their gasoline dollar, and also reduce environmental impacts, in the following ways:

- ensure that vehicles are properly tuned and lubricated
- maintain recommended tire inflation
- avoid sudden acceleration and obey speed limits
- avoid idling for more than 10 seconds outside of active traffic situations or minimum necessary winter warm-up
- choose the correct grade of gasoline, and
- compare fuel efficiency when buying vehicles.

Energy and You

Tap into the latest consumer news, energy savings tips, popular consumer and green tech resources and a weekly look at gasoline prices across the country on the Centre for Energy's *Flow*. Visit **www.centreflow.ca**

TAXES ON GASOLINE WHEN THE PUMP PRICE IS ONE DOLLAR PER LITRE
(cents per litre) as at January 1, 2009

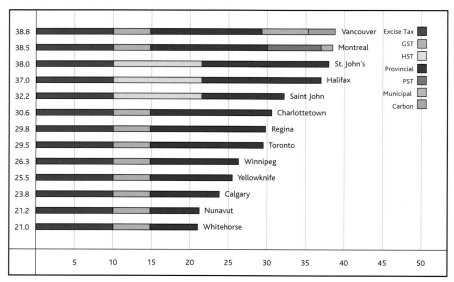

38.8	Vancouver
38.5	Montreal
38.0	St. John's
37.0	Halifax
32.2	Saint John
30.6	Charlottetown
29.8	Regina
29.5	Toronto
26.3	Winnipeg
25.5	Yellowknife
23.8	Calgary
21.2	Nunavut
21.0	Whitehorse

Legend: Excise Tax, GST, HST, Provincial, PST, Municipal, Carbon

Source: Natural Resources Canada

Section 3
Sustainable Development

The challenge

To remain sustainable —
economically, socially and
environmentally — the oil and gas
industry must continue to develop
new ways of doing things,
new ways of working with
stakeholders, and new products
to meet society's needs.

*"Sustainable development is
development that meets the
needs of the present without
compromising the ability
of future generations to meet
their own needs."*

– *Our Common Future*,
World Commission on Environment
and Development (Brundtland
Commission), 1987

*At the 1992 Conference on Environment and Development (termed the Earth
Summit), Canada and other members of the United Nations endorsed the
principle of sustainable development – a way of doing things that meets
people's current needs without damaging the prospects for future
generations. In practical terms, this means we must strive continuously to
protect and enhance both the environment and the economy. In 2002, at
a second Earth Summit in Johannesburg, South Africa, world leaders signaled
a shift in emphasis from broad goals to more detailed plans for putting
sustainable development into effect.*

*According to surveys by the United Nations and other organizations,
Canadians enjoy one of the highest standards of living on the planet.
Our comfortable lifestyles have been achieved despite harsh winters and
long distances between population centres. Much of our success is due to
reliable, convenient and affordable supplies of energy and products
obtained from crude oil and natural gas. Will this continue through the
21st century?*

*The oil and gas industry and governments at every level – local, regional,
national and international – are engaged in dialogue about environmental,
social and economic sustainability. People in government and industry
recognize that sustainable development must respect the views of the
stakeholders affected by policies, decisions and actions. Information and
education play an important role in these discussions by ensuring that
decisions are based on facts rather than mere opinions. Many companies,
governments, academics, non-government organizations and individuals
are working to meet this need.*

Minimizing impacts

The use of helicopter-portable seismic surveying has greatly reduced the impacts of exploration in forested and mountainous terrain.

Photo courtesy of EnCana

The environment

Every segment of the industry is addressing the local, regional and global environmental issues that arise from continued, and increased, production and use of crude oil and natural gas. The industry has made great strides in reducing its impacts on soil, water and wildlife during the past several decades. Air issues pose some of the biggest challenges to sustainability and are being addressed in many ways.

The oil and gas industry's key strategies for reducing impacts of air quality include improving the energy efficiency of operations and capturing more of the gases and vapours formerly released into the atmosphere. Similarly, the consumers of oil products and natural gas can do their part by purchasing more efficient vehicles and appliances. New vehicles, for example, release considerably fewer hydrocarbon vapours from fuel tanks and exhausts than equivalent older vehicles. End users of petroleum, as well as the producers, need to operate and maintain equipment responsibly.

Sulphur and nitrogen oxides and other emissions that contribute to acid rain and smog, and the greenhouse gases that affect global climate, are among the major air quality issues faced by the oil and gas industry. The industry's energy use and emissions per unit of production decreased in the 1990s, but this was offset by the major increase in total crude oil and natural gas output. Reducing greenhouse gas emissions is a major challenge facing the industry in the 21st century. Producing, processing and transporting crude oil and natural gas accounts for about one-sixth of Canada's energy-related greenhouse gas emissions. Companies representing more than 90 per cent of Canadian petroleum production have supported voluntary efforts to reduce these emissions.

For example, changes in equipment and procedures by natural gas production companies have greatly reduced the amount of methane released into the atmosphere. Government and industry are working together to reduce the amount of carbon dioxide released when unmarketable natural gas is flared during operations. Transmission pipelines have been curbing emissions by improving energy efficiency of facilities so that they consume less electricity and natural gas, and by reducing releases of methane into the atmosphere.

About two-thirds of Canadian crude oil demand is for motor vehicle fuels. Motor vehicle manufacturers are performing research and development on future vehicles that provide the same safety, comfort and capacity as today's vehicles but use one-third as much fuel. Canada's urban design, geography and population dispersal make it difficult to provide effective, efficient and economical mass transit options for many parts of the country. This decentralization means that motor vehicles are likely to remain a dominant feature of transportation systems outside the major metropolitan areas.

CANADIAN MOTOR VEHICLE EFFICIENCY IN 2005
(litres per 100 kilometres)

Age of vehicles	Light Vehicles (gasoline)	Medium Trucks (diesel)	Heavy Trucks (diesel)
2 and less	10.6	23.3	33.6
3 to 5	10.0	25.8	35.2
6 to 9	10.6	28.3	35.3
10 to 13	10.7	30.0	38.2
14 and over	12.4	36.7	43.4

Source: Natural Resources Canada

REFERENCE CASE DIRECT EMISSIONS PROJECTION
(million tonnes of CO_2e per year)

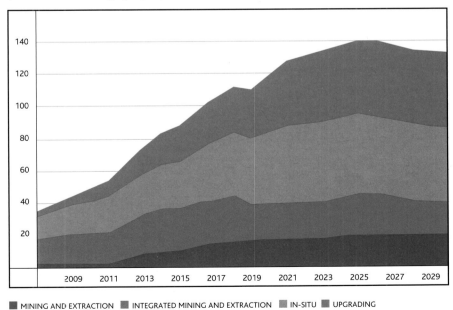

■ MINING AND EXTRACTION ■ INTEGRATED MINING AND EXTRACTION ■ IN-SITU ■ UPGRADING

Source: Canadian Energy Research Institute

The direct emissions are shown above, and not surprisingly rise along with the projected increase in oil sands production and natural gas use.

Photo courtesy of Syncrude Canada Ltd.

Where the wood bison roam

In oil sands mining, clean sand from the processing facility is returned to mined-out areas. Fast-growing grass – using species native to the area wherever possible – is used to stabilize the surface of the reclaimed land, and some of this land is replanted with trees. In one research project, wood bison now graze on reclaimed land following oil sands mining.

The effect of motor vehicles on the environment will depend on how rapidly science and technology can produce more efficient models, what vehicles people choose to buy, and how much they drive. Alternative vehicle fuels from renewable sources such as ethanol or biodiesel are being developed, but the volumes produced are still a small fraction of the amount needed to displace gasoline and diesel fuel.

The other environmental issues facing the oil and gas industry – such as protecting biological diversity, maintaining soil and water resources and preventing toxic releases – are more localized but no less vital to sustainable development. There are encouraging developments in each of these areas.

Biological diversity is being addressed through narrower seismic cutlines, made possible by new technologies. Surrounding vegetation grows back more quickly over a two-metre corridor than over a five-metre swath. This is important because cutlines, like other linear clearings, can provide corridors for predators, hunters and recreational vehicles that disrupt forest ecosystems. Other advances in biodiversity conservation include greater use of native species for reclamation and scheduling oil and gas industry activities to avoid wildlife mating and nesting seasons.

Industry has also made progress toward reducing the amount of timber it cuts. The area cleared for well pad installations has been reduced by about 40 per cent compared to the 1970s, and drilling multiple wells from a single pad has become commonplace.

Co-operative planning between forest and energy companies, called integrated landscape management, reduces the number of roads required by both industries and reduces the effects of oil and gas development on forest growth and yield.

Extensive studies of marine ecosystems are now required before any offshore oil and natural gas activity. The effects of projects are monitored during the work and afterwards, and negative effects are rapidly addressed. Joint advisory bodies between the fishing and petroleum industries also help to ensure effects on marine resources are minimized.

The pipeline and oil sands mining sectors have been improving their techniques for restoring and replanting rights-of-way and surface mines. One key measure is stripping topsoil and stockpiling it separately for replacement over mineral soil. Scientists continue to improve techniques for monitoring soil contamination and using bacteria and fertilizers to restore soil quality.

Government and industry continue to develop new ways to reduce the amount of water used by conventional oil and gas activities and oil sands projects. Greater recycling has already reduced the industry's water requirements considerably. New options include using treatment facilities to process wastewater so that it does not have to be injected into deep disposal wells, and using non-potable water whenever possible.

New regulations for workplaces and transportation in the 1990s led to big improvements in the way that hazardous materials are handled in the oil and gas industry, reducing the likelihood that workers or the public would be exposed to toxic substances. In many instances, companies found ways to reduce or eliminate their use of hazardous substances. A new national reporting system allows government and the public to monitor hazardous releases into the environment.

New challenges continue to arise, of course. There is, for example, a new focus on the "cumulative effects" of multiple projects and industries on an area's residents and ecosystems. The oil sands area around Fort McMurray has been pioneering new ways to monitor and address cumulative effects. Another emerging issue is "encroachment," which occurs when one land use (such as residential or recreational development) moves into an area where another land use (such as oil and gas production) is already well established.

The economy

To remain sustainable economically, the Canadian oil and gas industry needs to be efficient and competitive on a global scale. It will take investment and innovation to meet ever-rising environmental expectations, regulatory requirements and the needs of present and future generations of consumers.

In 2007, crude oil and natural gas provided 67 per cent of the energy used by Canadians. Petrochemicals derived from crude oil and natural gas are made into thousands of products. The oil and gas industry is a major employer and a vital component of the economy.

In 2007, the Canadian petroleum industry supplied about $50 billion worth of crude oil and equivalents, natural gas and refined oil products to meet our petroleum-based energy and petrochemical needs. Without the industry, we would have had to spend at least as much on imported supplies. In addition, Canada received about $50 billion in revenues from petroleum and natural gas exports in 2007.

The oil and gas industry has become much more efficient and able to respond to fluctuations in crude oil and natural gas prices. New technologies have created new opportunities, and Canadian expertise often finds profitable applications abroad.

As U.S. petroleum supplies decline and become more costly to find and produce, Canada finds ready markets for increased production of natural gas, bitumen, heavy oil, conventional oil and natural gas liquids from both Western Canada and new East Coast offshore projects. Expanded pipeline systems give producers access to markets across the continent. Arctic pipelines could open up new

development opportunities for Canadian oil and gas companies and for northern residents.

Natural gas continues to play an increasingly important role in the North American energy economy. In addition to natural gas reserves already discovered in Western Canada, and under development off the East Coast, large supplies have been discovered in the Arctic. Development of northern natural gas resources requires successful conclusion of regulatory processes, community consultation and environmental assessment, but becomes more attractive when natural gas prices are high enough to support the construction of pipelines to southern markets.

People who work in the oil and gas industry – like the government officials who establish and enforce regulations – are also citizens, parents and consumers. Sustainable development is both a long-term goal and an ongoing process. It requires continuing discussion and analysis. As science, technology, economics and social values evolve, so will the role of the Canadian petroleum industry.

Through the goods and services they buy, consumers will influence many of the key decisions about the future of crude oil and natural gas. Where Canadians live and work, the standard of living they require, what recreation they choose – these will be major factors determining the demand for energy and petrochemicals. In addition, governments respond to public demands as they set policies that play a critical role in establishing the regulatory framework in which the oil and gas industry operates.

Society's role

Science and technology also affect decision-making about the uses of crude oil and natural gas. If ways are found to use these fuels more cleanly and efficiently, the petroleum era could extend through the 21st century and beyond. Non-energy uses of crude oil and natural gas, to make everything from pavement to plastics, will certainly continue far into the future.

Natural gas and oil products will be the most efficient and economical means to meet many human needs for decades to come. They have been described as "transition fuels" on the road to a future less dependent on non-renewable resources. However, it is unclear how known alternatives – nuclear fission, hydroelectricity, wind and solar energy, for example – could provide all the goods and services now obtained from petroleum. Canadians certainly want to continue enjoying the benefits of competitively priced energy.

The way each society achieves sustainable development depends or its natural circumstances and a combination of science, technology, economics and social values. Science helps us to identify both problems and solutions. Technology gives us the tools to get things done. The economy provides the means to buy the technology and pay the scientists, engineers and other workers. Social values determine our economic and environmental priorities.

Society's values are perhaps the most difficult factor to gauge and judge. However, companies and governments are making unprecedented efforts across Canada to consult with affected individuals and interest groups about both specific energy projects and the broader directions of energy policies.

The planet's human population has doubled in the past half-century and, based on current trends, could grow another 50 per cent sometime in this century. Billions of people aspire to a high standard of living like that enjoyed by Canadians today. By learning how to use crude oil and natural gas wisely and more efficiently and by providing more goods and services with fewer environmental impacts, Canadians can improve their quality of life while developing highly marketable knowledge and technologies. Accomplishing this daunting and costly task could yield great benefits for the individuals and companies involved as well as for society as a whole.

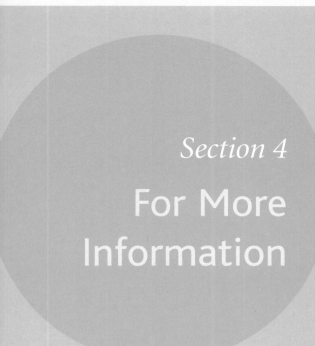

Section 4
For More Information

Photo courtesy of Syncrude Canada Ltd.

Did you know?

The barrel is a common unit of measurement in the Canadian and international crude oil industries. It is based on the wooden barrels used to store and transport crude oil in the 19th century.

Measurement

Crude oil, natural gas liquids and refined oil products

In metric, oil and gas are measured in cubic metres (m^3), (Système International or SI), simply the volume of fluid held by a container with dimensions of one metre by one metre by one metre.

The standard North American unit of oil measurement is the barrel (bbl), which holds 159 litres or 42 U.S. gallons. A standard bathtub holds about one barrel of oil.

Volumes of gasoline and motor oils are normally measured in litres in Canada, and in U.S. gallons and quarts in the United States.

Liquid measurement conversions

All liquid petroleum measurement in North America – including crude oil, gasoline, diesel, jet fuel and heating oil – is temperature corrected to a standard 15° C at sea-level atmospheric pressure.

To convert from:	To:	Multiply by:
Cubic metre	Barrel	6.292
Barrel	Cubic metre	0.15891
Litre	Barrel	0.006292
Barrel	Litre	158.91
Litre	Cubic metre	0.001
Cubic metre	Litre	1000.0

Other conversions

1 kilogram	=	2.2 pounds
1 metre	=	3.28 feet
1 kilometre	=	0.62 miles
1 centimetre	=	0.4 inches
1 hectare	=	2.47 acres
1 U.S. gallon	=	3.79 litres
1 Imperial gallon	=	4.55 litres
1 barrel	=	35 Imperial gallons/42 U.S. gallons

In the U.S. and Imperial systems, energy content is measured in British Thermal Units (BTUs). One BTU is the heat required to raise the temperature of one pound of water one degree Fahrenheit.

Natural gas measurement conversions

To convert from:	To:	Multiply by:
Cubic metre	Cubic foot	35.301
Cubic foot	Cubic metre	0.028
1,000 cubic metres (10^3 m^3)	Million cubic feet (MMcf)	0.035
Million cubic feet (MMcf)	1,000 cubic metres (10^3 m^3)	28.328
Joule	BTU	0.00095
BTU	joule	1054.615
Gigajoule	Million BTUs (MMBTU)	0.948
Million BTUs (MMBTU)	Gigajoule	1.055

Natural gas

In SI, the official basic unit for natural gas volume measurement is one thousand cubic metres (10^3 m^3), measured at standard temperature and pressure (15° C, 101.325 kilopascals.)

The space taken up by a large office desk is almost one cubic metre. This amount of gas would heat water for about 600 cups of coffee.

The following units and abbreviations are commonly used:

1 thousand cubic metres = 10^3 m^3
Energy used by one water heater for a year

1 million cubic metres = 10^6 m^3
Enough to heat 180 homes for one year*

1 billion cubic metres = 10^9 m^3
Enough to heat 180,000 homes for one year*

In the U.S. and Imperial systems, the basic unit for natural gas volume measurement is the cubic foot (cf) measured at standard temperature and pressure (60° Fahrenheit, 14.73 pounds per square inch). Common multiples are one thousand cubic feet (Mcf), one million cubic feet (MMcf), one billion cubic feet (Bcf) and one trillion cubic feet (Tcf).

Energy

The joule is the basic SI unit used to measure energy content. One joule is the equivalent of the energy required to heat one gram of water by approximately one quarter of one degree Celsius, or to lift a 100-gram object (such as a television remote control) one metre vertically. Since the joule is such a small unit of energy, the natural gas industry normally works in large multiples. Completely burning one wooden match would release the equivalent of approximately 1,000 joules.

1 thousand joules (10^3 J)	=	1 kJ (kilojoule)
1 million joules (10^6 J)	=	1 MJ (megajoule)
1 billion joules (10^9 J)	=	1 GJ (gigajoule)
1 trillion joules (10^{12} J)	=	1 TJ (terajoule)
1 million gigajoules (10^{15} J)	=	1 PJ (petajoule)
410 MJs	=	Used by one home in a day*
150 GJs	=	Used by one home in a year*

*Varies according to house size and weather conditions.

Reviewers

The following individuals have generously provided their time and expertise to assist in the development of this publication:

Bob Arefi
Southern Alberta Institute of Technology

Bill Ayrton
Ayrton Exploration Ltd.

Bruce Cameron
Nova Scotia Department of Energy

Suzanne Clément-Cousineau, Philip Jennings
and Maureen Monaghan
Natural Resources Canada

Roger Connelly
Inuvialuit Regional Corporation

Bruce DeBaie
Enbridge Inc.

Onno DeVries, Stephen Rodrigues and Ian Scott
Canadian Association of Petroleum Producers

Michael Ervin and Cathy Hay
M.J. Ervin & Associates

Geoff Granville and Simone Marler
Shell Canada Limited

Tom Hegan
Rimbey and Area District Clean Air People (RADCAP)

Ross Hicks
National Energy Board

William Kerr
Canadian Energy Pipeline Association

Lynn Lehr
Chevron Canada Resources

Eric Lloyd
Petroleum Technology Alliance Canada

Tony Pargeter
Petro-Canada

Andy Pickard
Consultant

Randy Provencal
Syncrude Canada Ltd.

Bill Reynen
Environment Canada

Barbara Riley
Nova Scotia Community College

Colin White
Keyano College

The following individuals provided comments and revisions for the fifth printing of this publication:

Connor Bays
Canadian Energy Pipeline Association

Colleen Brown
Enbridge Inc.

Suzanne Clément-Cousineau
Natural Resources Canada

Roger Connelly
Inuvialuit Regional Corporation

Cathy Hay
M.J. Ervin & Associates

Simone Marler
Shell Canada Limited

Stephen Rodrigues
Canadian Association of Petroleum Producers

Selected bibliography

The following references provide additional information about the Canadian and international petroleum industries:

Baker, Ron. *A Primer of Oilwell Drilling*. 5th ed. The University of Texas at Austin, Petroleum Extension Service, 1997.

Berger, Bill D. and Kenneth E. Anderson, Ph.D. *Modern Petroleum – A Basic Primer of the Industry*. Tulsa: PennWell Publishing Company, 1992.

Bott, Robert. *Mileposts: The Story of the World's Longest Pipeline*. Edmonton: Interprovincial Pipe Line, 1989.

Breen, David H. *Alberta's Petroleum Industry and the Conservation Board*. Edmonton: The University of Alberta Press, 1993.

Bryson, Connie, ed. *Opportunity Oil Sands*. Winnipeg: Fleet Publications Inc., 1996.

de Mille, George. *Oil in Canada West: The Early Years*. Calgary: George de Mille, 1969.

Finch, David, Peter McKenzie-Brown and Gordon Jaremko. *The Great Oil Age*. Calgary: Detselig Publishers, 1993.

Hyne, Norman J. *Nontechnical Guide to Petroleum Geology, Exploration, Drilling and Production*. Tulsa: PennWell Publishing Company, 1995.

Langenkamp, Robert D. *The Illustrated Petroleum Reference Dictionary*. 4th ed. Tulsa: PennWell Publishing Company, 1994.

Leffler, William L. *Petroleum Refining for the Nontechnical Person*. 2nd ed. PennWell Publishing Company, 1985.

McCann, T.J., and Phil Magee. "Crude Oil Greenhouse Gas Life Cycle Analysis Helps Assign Values For CO2 Emissions Trading," *The Oil and Gas Journal*. Tulsa, February 22, 1999.

Stahl, Len. *A Record of Service: The History of Western Canada's Pioneer Gas and Electric Utilities*. Edmonton: Canadian Utilities Limited, 1987.

Stenson, Fred. *Waste to Wealth: A History of Gas Processing in Canada*. Calgary: Canadian Gas Processors Association, 1985.

The Royal Tyrrell Museum of Palaentology. *The Land Before Us – The Making of Ancient Alberta*. Red Deer College Press, 1994.

Van Dyke, Kate. *Fundamentals of Petroleum*. 4th ed. Austin: The University of Texas at Austin, Petroleum Extension Service, 1997.

Yergin, Daniel. *The Prize*. New York: Simon & Schuster, 1991.

Other information sources

The Canadian Centre for Energy Information (www.centreforenergy.com) provides an overview of the Canadian oil and natural gas industry and links to hundreds of additional sites with up-to-date information about the Canadian and international energy sector.

The annual reports of companies, associations, regulatory agencies and government departments provide current information about their activities, plans and environmental programs. Many of these reports can be viewed on the Internet and reached through links on the Centre for Energy portal. Among the annual reports used in preparing this edition of *Our Petroleum Challenge*:

- Alberta Utilities Commission
- Alberta Energy Resource Conservation Board
- Canada-Newfoundland and Labrador Offshore Petroleum Board
- Canada-Nova Scotia Offshore Petroleum Board
- Canadian Association of Petroleum Producers
- Canadian Energy Pipeline Association
- Canadian Petroleum Products Institute
- Canadian Gas Association
- Canadian Association of Oilwell Drilling Contractors
- Canadian Chemical Producers Association
- Environment Canada
- National Energy Board
- Natural Resources Canada
- Petroleum Services Association of Canada
- Transportation Safety Board of Canada

BP Statistical Review of World Energy is an authoritative source of international energy information, published annually in London, England, by the British Petroleum Company. It is also available on the Internet at www.bp.com.

This publication is provided for educational purposes only and the Canadian Centre for Energy Information makes no representation about the results to be obtained from using this publication or the accuracy, reliability, completeness or currency of the content. In no event will the Canadian Centre for Energy Information, or any parties contributing content to this publication, be liable to you for damages, of any kind, based upon any cause of action or theory, arising out of your use of this publication. The Canadian Centre for Energy Information does not endorse any product, service, or process which may be described in this publication.

Glossary

A

Abandoned well: A well that is permanently shut down because it has ceased to produce crude oil or natural gas or because it was a dry hole.

Abandonment: Converting a drilled well to a condition that can be left indefinitely without further attention and will not damage freshwater supplies, potential petroleum reservoirs or the environment.

Acidizing: The injection of acids under pressure into the rock formation to create channels that allow the hydrocarbons to flow more easily into the wellbore.

Acid rain: Natural rain or snow containing sulphuric acid and nitric acid which is created when industrial pollutants, especially sulphur dioxide and nitrogen oxides, undergo chemical changes in the atmosphere.

Air drilling: The use of compressed air instead of mud as a drilling fluid to remove the cuttings; air drilling increases penetration rates but offers no control over downhole gas pressure on water in the subsurface formations or downhole gas pressure.

Allowables: The rate of production for a well or group of wells that is set by a regulatory authority (conservation commission).

Alternative fuels: Other fuels that can be substituted for the fuel in use. In the case of natural gas, the most common alternative fuels are distillate fuel oils, residual fuel oils, coal and wood.

Annulus: The space between two concentric lengths of pipe or between pipe and the hole in which it is located.

Associated gas: Gas that is produced from the same reservoir along with crude oil, either as free gas or in solution.

B

Backhaul: A transaction that results in natural gas being "transported" in the opposite direction of the physical flow of a transportation system. This is usually achieved by redelivering the gas at a point upstream from the point of receipt.

Backstopping: A service that provides alternate supplies of natural gas in the event that a consumer's gas is not delivered.

Barrel: The common unit for measuring petroleum. One barrel contains approximately 159 litres.

Benchmark crude: See *Marker crude.*

Benzene: A volatile organic compound that occurs naturally in petroleum and is also produced by the combustion of petroleum products.

Bitumen: Petroleum that exists in the semisolid or solid phase in natural deposits; a thick, sticky form of crude oil that must be heated or diluted before it will flow into a well or through a pipeline.

Blowout: An uncontrolled flow of gas, oil or other fluids from a well.

Blowout preventer (BOP): Equipment that is installed at the wellhead to control pressures and fluids during drilling, completion and certain remedial operations to restore production.

Bonus payment: The amount paid at land auctions for Crown mineral rights.

BOP stack: Several blowout preventers used in combination.

British thermal unit (BTU): The quantity of heat required to raise the temperature of one pound of water by one degree Fahrenheit at or near 39.2^O Fahrenheit.

Broker: An individual or independent corporation engaged in bringing together sellers and buyers of natural gas, assisting in negotiations, arranging transportation and delivery terms. Brokers usually do not buy or sell for their own account but act as agent for the buyer and/or seller.

Bundled service: A service provided by a pipeline or a local distribution company which includes the natural gas as well as all the necessary services required for a consistent supply (backstopping, load balancing, storage).

Burner-tip: The point of end-use consumption of a particular fuel, such as natural gas or residual fuel oil.

Burner-tip price: The price of natural gas (or other fuels) paid by the final consumer: for natural gas, this includes the price of the gas plus the cost of processing, gathering, transmitting and distributing it.

C

Cable-tool drilling: One of two principal methods of drilling for crude oil and natural gas. Cable-tool drilling is the older method and consists of raising and dropping a heavy drill bit, suspended from the end of a cable, so that it pounds and pulverizes its way through the subsurface structures. Water in the hole keeps the cuttings in suspension for removal at regular intervals by bailing.

Cap rock: The impervious geological rock that overlays the reservoir rock and traps natural gas or crude oil in the reservoir; also called "sealing rock."

Carbonate: Rock formed from the hard parts of marine organisms, mainly consisting of calcite, aragonite and dolomite.

Carbon dioxide (CO_2): A non-toxic gas produced from decaying materials, respiration of plant and animal life, and combustion of organic matter, including fossil fuels; carbon dioxide is the most common greenhouse gas produced by human activities.

Casing: A type of pipe that is used for encasing a smaller diameter carrier pipe for installation in a well. The casing prevents the wall from caving in and protects against ground water contamination and uncontrolled hydrocarbon releases. See also *surface casing*.

Casing-head gasoline (naphtha): A highly volatile liquid that is separated from natural gas at the wellhead and was once used as unrefined gasoline.

Cat cracking (catalytic cracking): A refinery process that uses catalysts in addition to pressure and heat to convert heavier fuel oil into lighter products such as gasoline and diesel fuel.

Catalysts: Materials that assist chemical reactions.

Cathodic protection: A technique for preventing corrosion in metal pipelines and tanks that uses weak electric currents to offset the current associated with metal corrosion.

Centrifugal pump: A rotating pump, commonly used for large-volume oil and natural gas pipelines, that takes in fluids near the centre and accelerates them as they move to the outlet on the outer rim.

Christmas tree: The valve assembly at the top of tubing strings and casing of a natural gas well (or a free-flowing crude oil well) to provide primary pressure reduction, production rate control and shut-in capabilities.

City-gate: The delivery point or the point of interconnection between long-distance transmission pipelines (usually interprovincial or interstate) and local distribution companies.

Clastic: Made up of pieces (clasts) of older rock; rock derived from mechanical process; generally sandstone, siltstone or shale.

Coalbed methane: Natural gas generated and trapped in coal seams. In Canada, now called natural gas from coal (NGC).

Coal gas: A mixture of hydrogen, carbon monoxide and methane, produced by distilling coal, that was once used for heating and lighting.

Co-firing: The process of burning natural gas in conjunction with another fuel.

Cogeneration: The simultaneous production of electricity and steam from one energy source (e.g., natural gas, oil, biomass).

Coiled tubing: A continuous, jointless hollow steel cylinder that is stored on a reel and can be uncoiled or coiled repeatedly as required; coiled tubing is increasingly being used in well completion and servicing instead of traditional tubing, which is made up of joined sections of pipe.

Coke: Solid carbon that remains in the refining process after cracking of hydrocarbons.

Coking: A process used to break down heavy oil molecules into lighter ones by removing the carbon which remains as a coke residue.

Combined-cycle generation: When the steam generated in a cogeneration process is used to create additional electricity. In this way, the efficiency of producing electricity is increased.

Commingled gas: A homogeneous mix of natural gas from various physical (or contractual) sources.

Common depth point method: A method of recording and processing seismic signals so that signals belonging to the same subsurface point are brought together.

Completion: The process of finishing a well so that it is ready to produce oil or gas.

Compressed natural gas (CNG): Natural gas that has been highly compressed and is stored in high-pressure surface containers. CNG is used as a transportation fuel for automobiles, trucks and busses.

Compressor: A machine used to boost natural gas pressure to move it through pipelines or other facilities.

Compressor station: Permanent facilities containing compressors that supply the energy needed to move natural gas at increased pressures.

Condensate: Hydrocarbons, usually produced with natural gas, which are liquid at normal pressure and temperature.

Consumption: The quantity of natural gas used by final consumers.

Conventional crude oil: Oil produced by drilling wells and, if necessary, pumping – methods used in the petroleum industry since the 19th century. Conventional oil is generally liquid at room temperature.

Conventional gas: Natural gas that can be produced using recovery techniques normally employed by the oil and gas industry. The distinction between conventional and unconventional gas is becoming less clear. See also *unconventional gas*.

Core: A continuous cylinder of rock, usually from five to 10 centimetres in diameter, cut from the bottom of a wellbore as a sample of an underground formation.

Cracking: A refining process for increasing the yield of gasoline from crude oil; cracking involves breaking down the larger, heavier and more complex hydrocarbon molecules into simpler and lighter molecules through the use of heat and pressure, and sometimes a catalyst.

Critical sour gas wells: A sour gas well that has the potential to release unsafe levels of hydrogen sulphide, which might affect nearby residents.

Critical zone: The zone in a well where sour gas will likely be encountered.

Crown land: Mineral rights that are owned by the federal or provincial governments in Canada.

Crude oil: A naturally occurring liquid mixture of hydrocarbons trapped in underground rock.

Cubic foot: The volume of gas that fills a cube that is one foot by one foot by one foot under set temperature and pressure conditions. The standard pressure is 14.73 pounds per square inch (101.6 Kilopascals) and the standard temperature is 60 degrees Fahrenheit (15.56° Celcius).

Cuttings: Chips and small fragments of rock cut by the drill bit and brought to the surface by the flow of drilling mud fluid. See also *horizontal drilling* and *horizontal wells*.

D

Darcy: A measure of rock permeability (i.e., the degree to which natural gas and crude oil can move through the rocks).

Deep basin gas: Gas that is found at depths greater than the average for a particular area.

Deliverability: The amount of natural gas a well, field, gathering, transmission or distribution system can supply in a given period of time.

Density: The heaviness of crude oil, indicating the proportion of large, carbon-rich molecules, generally measured in kilograms per cubic metre (kg/m3) or degrees on the American Petroleum Institute (API) gravity scale; in Western Canada oil up to 900 kg/m3 is considered light to medium crude – oil above this density is deemed as heavy oil or bitumen.

Deregulation: The process of changing natural gas market regulations to allow a greater role for market forces to balance supply and demand and set prices. It does not mean the absence of regulation.

Derrick: A load-bearing tower-like structure over a natural gas or crude oil well that holds the hoisting and lowering equipment for drilling, testing and reworking wells.

Desiccant: Any absorbent or adsorbent (liquid or solid) that will remove water or water vapour from a material.

Desulphurization: The process of removing sulphur and sulphur compounds from gases or liquid hydrocarbon mixes.

Development well: A well drilled in or adjacent to a proven part of a pool to optimize petroleum production.

Diluents: Light petroleum liquids used to dilute bitumen and heavy oil so they can flow through pipelines.

Directional drilling: Controlled drilling at a specified angle from the vertical.

Directional (deviated) well: A well drilled at an angle from the vertical by using a slanted drilling rig or by deflecting the drill bit; directional wells are used to drill multiple wells from a common drilling pad or to reach a subsurface location beneath land or water where drilling cannot be done.

Discovery well: Exploratory well that discovers a new gas or oil field.

Dolomite: Sedimentary rock rich in calcium carbonate and magnesium in which oil or gas reservoirs are often found. See also *limestone*.

Downstream: The refining and marketing sector of the petroleum industry.

Drawworks: The hoisting mechanism on a drilling rig which spools off or takes in the drilling line and thus raises or lowers the drill string and bit.

Drilling mud: Fluid circulated down the drill pipe and up the annulus during drilling to remove cuttings, cool and lubricate the bit, and maintain desired pressure in the well.

Drill pipe: Steel pipe sections, approximately 9.5 meters long, that are screwed together to form a continuous pipe extending from the drilling rig to the drilling bit at the bottom of the hole. Rotation of the drill pipe and bit causes the bit to bore through the rock.

Drillstem test: A method of sampling fluid from a formation using a tool attached to the drillstem; the sample is used to assess the type and volume of fluids in the formation as well as their pressure and rate of flow.

Drill string: A column or string of drill pipe. The drill string carries the mud down to, and rotates, the drill bit.

Dry gas: Natural gas from the well that is free of liquid hydrocarbons, or gas that has been treated to remove all liquids; pipeline gas.

Dry hole: An unsuccessful well; a well not capable of producing commercial quantities of oil or gas.

E

Electric well log: A record of electrical characteristics of formations that have been drilled through. Electric logs are used to identify the formations, determine the nature and amount of fluids they contain, and estimate their depth.

Enhanced oil recovery (EOR): Any method that increases oil production by using techniques or materials that are not part of normal pressure maintenance or water flooding operations. For example, natural gas can be injected into a reservoir to "enhance" or increase oil production.

Established reserves: Those reserves recoverable under current technology and present and anticipated economic conditions.

Exploration: The act of searching for potential subsurface reservoirs of gas or oil. Methods include the use of magnetometers, gravity meters, seismic exploration, surface mapping, and exploratory drilling.

Exploratory well: A well drilled either in search of a new, as yet undiscovered accumulation of oil and gas, or in an attempt to significantly extend the limits of a known reservoir.

Extraction loss: The reduction in volume of natural gas resulting from the removal of the natural gas liquid constituents at the processing plant. See also *shrinkage*.

F

Farmout: An arrangement whereby the owner of a lease assigns some portion (or all) of the lease to another company for drilling.

Field: The geographical area encompassing a group of one or more underground petroleum pools sharing the same or related infrastructure.

Field pressure: The pressure of the natural gas as it is found in the underground formations from which it is produced.

Field price: The amount received by petroleum producers after deducting transportation and distribution costs.

Fish: An object left in the well bore during drilling or workover operations that must be recovered or drilled around before work can proceed.

Fishing: The term encompasses both the special equipment and the special procedures required to remove undesirable objects from the well bore.

Formation: A designated subsurface layer that is composed throughout of substantially the same kind of rock or rock types.

Fracturing (or fracing): The practice of pumping special fluids down the well under high pressure; fracturing causes the formation to crack open, creating passages for the reservoir fluids to flow more easily into the wellbore.

G

Gas: One of the three states of matter: liquid, solid and gas. Gas is characterized by the fact that it has neither shape nor specific volume: it expands to fill the entire container in which it is held.

Gas cap: A layer of free gas on top of the oil zone in an underground reservoir.

Gas controller: A person or persons who are responsible for monitoring and controlling daily gas system operations and ensuring safety of a gathering, transmission or distribution system.

Gas cycling: A petroleum recovery process that takes produced gas and condensate and injects it back into the reservoir to increase pressure and increase the production of natural gas liquids. See also *repressuring*.

Gas hydrates: Crystals of water and methane molecules found in vast quantities on ocean floors and in the Arctic.

Gas in place (GIP): The volume of gas in a reservoir at any given time, calculated at standard temperature and pressure conditions, including both recoverable and nonrecoverable gas.

Gas meter: An instrument that measures (and may record) the volume of gas that has passed through it.

Gas pool: The term "pool" is generally synonymous with the term "reservoir".

Gas processing plant: Any facility which performs one or more of the following: removing liquefiable hydrocarbons from wet gas or casinghead gas; removing undesirable gaseous and particulate elements from natural gas; removing water or moisture from the gas stream.

Gas reservoir: A rock stratum that forms a trap for the accumulation of crude oil and natural gas.

Gas transmission systems: Pipelines that carry natural gas at high pressure from producing areas to consuming areas.

Gasification: The process of turning liquefied natural gas into a vapourous or gaseous state by increasing the temperature and decreasing the pressure.

Gasoline: A complex mixture of relatively volatile hydrocarbons, with or without small quantities of additives suitable for use in spark-ignition engines.

Gathering lines: Pipelines that move raw petroleum from wellheads to processing plants and transmission facilities.

Gathering system: A system of pipelines, compressor stations and other related facilities that gather natural gas from the supply region and transport it to the major transmission systems.

Geochemistry: The science of chemistry applied to rocks and minerals; geochemists analyze the contents of subsurface rocks for the presence of organic matter associated with oil deposits.

Geological trap: Any geological structure that stops the migration of natural gas, crude oil and water through subsurface rocks, causing the hydrocarbons to accumulate into pools in the reservoir rock.

Geologist: A person trained in the study of the Earth's crust; petroleum geologists search for traps that could contain petroleum, recommend drilling locations and analyse drilling results.

Geophones (or jugs): Sensitive vibration-detecting instruments used in conducting seismic surveys; marine versions are known as hydrophones.

Geophysical survey: Searching and mapping the subsurface structure of the earth's crust using geophysical methods to locate probable reservoir structures capable of producing commercial quantities of natural gas and/or crude oil.

Geophysics: The science that deals with the relations between the physical features of the Earth and forces that produce them; geophysics includes the study of seismology and magnetism.

Greenhouse effect: The warming of the Earth's surface caused by the presence of carbon dioxide and other gases in the atmosphere that trap the heat of the sun.

Greenhouse gases: A wide variety of gases that trap heat near the Earth's surface, preventing its escape into space; greenhouse gases, such as carbon dioxide, methane, nitrous oxide and water vapour, occur naturally or result from human activities such as the burning of fossil fuels.

Ground-level ozone: See *volatile organic compounds*.

Gun perforator: A device that creates small holes through the casing, cement and into the producing formation of a well. The holes provide channels for gas and/or crude oil to flow into the well.

Gusher: A well that comes in with such great pressure that the oil or gas blows out of the wellhead like a geyser; gushers are rare today because of improved drilling technology, especially the use of drilling mud to control downhole pressure.

H

Heavy oil: Dense, viscous oil, with a high proportion of bitumen, which is difficult to extract with conventional techniques and is more costly to transport and refine.

Horizontal drilling: Drilling a well that deviates from the vertical and travels horizontally through a producing layer.

Horizontal laterals: A series of drainage wells branching off from a horizontal wellbore.

Hot water process: A method for separating bitumen from oil sand using hot water and caustic soda, developed by Karl Clark of the Alberta Research Council.

Hydrocarbons: A large class of liquid, solid or gaseous organic compounds, containing only carbon and hydrogen, which are the basis of almost all petroleum products.

Hydrocracking: A refining process which adds hydrogen to the carbon-rich molecules of heavier oil, in the presence of a catalyst, to produce a higher proportion of gasoline and diesel fuel.

Hydrogen sulphide (H_2S): A naturally occurring, highly toxic gas with the odour of rotten eggs.

Hydrotransport: A process that uses hot water to transport oil sand through a pipeline to a processing plant.

Hydrotreating: The process of adding hydrogen to heavy oil or bitumen molecules during the upgrading process.

I

Infill drilling: Wells drilled between established producing wells on a lease in order to increase production from the reservoir.

Infill well: Any well that is drilled on a closer-than-normal well spacing pattern or requirement. Also, any well drilled between existing wells producing from the same reservoir.

Injection well: A well used for injecting air, steam or fluids into an underground formation.

Inorganic theory: A theory that maintains petroleum originated from hydrocarbons that were trapped inside the Earth during the planet's formation and are slowly moving upwards.

In-situ: In its original place; in position; in-situ recovery refers to various methods used to recover deeply buried bitumen deposits, including steam injection, solvent injection and firefloods.

Intervenor: A person, business entity or other organization that is granted the right to participate in a regulatory hearing.

J

Jackknife or folding mast: The type of mast that can be folded for moving, as opposed to the standard derrick, which has to be completely dismantled and re-erected.

Joint implementation: A means of reducing global greenhouse gas emissions whereby a country receives credit for supporting emissions reductions elsewhere – for example, planting trees or replacing inefficient power generation facilities in developing countries.

K

Kelly: The first and sturdiest joint of the drill string in conventional rotary drilling rigs; a thick-walled, hollow steel forging with four flat sides that fits into a square hole in the rotary table.

Kerosene: A mixture of hydrocarbons produced by distilling petroleum, which is used as a lamp oil or jet fuel.

Kick: When fluids with a higher pressure than that exerted by the drilling mud enter the wellbore; this creates the potential for a well to blow out of control.

L

Land: In the petroleum industry, "land" often refers to the oil and gas rights on a particular area of land. For example, in a "land sale," the oil and/or gas rights are "sold" (although in reality the rights are leased).

Landman: A male or female member or the exploration team whose primary duties are formulating and carrying out exploration strategies and managing an oil company's relations with its landowners and partners, including securing and administering oil and gas leases and other agreements. Also known as a land agent or land person.

Lease: An agreement between two or more parties where the owner of the surface and/or mineral rights grants another party the right to drill and produce petroleum substances in exchange for payment.

Light crude oil: Liquid petroleum which has a low density and flows freely at room temperature.

Limestone: Calcium carbonate-rich sedimentary rocks in which oil or gas reservoirs are often found.

Linepack: The volume of gas which is needed to be kept in the pipe of a gathering, transmission or distribution system in order to ensure the functioning of the system. Linepack can sometimes be used for short-term temporary storage of additional gas supplies.

Liquefied natural gas (LNG): Supercooled natural gas that is maintained as a liquid at or below -160°C; LNG occupies 1/640th of its original volume and is therefore easier to transport if pipelines cannot be used.

Logs: Detailed depth-related records of certain significant details of an oil or gas well; usually obtained by lowering measurement instruments into a well.

Looping: A method of increasing capacity on a pipeline: an existing pipeline by another line over any part or the whole length of the original pipeline.

M

Main: A distribution line that serves as a common source of supply for more than one service line. Its dimensions and operating pressure can be similar to those in a transmission system.

Manufactured gas: A gas obtained by destructive distillation of coal, by the thermal decomposition of oil, or by the reaction of steam passing through a bed of heated coal or coke. Examples are coal gases, coke or oven gases, producer gas, blast furnace gas, blue (water) gas, or carbureted water gas.

Marker crude: A specific crude oil, usually a blended crude of defined properties, used as a reference for pricing other crude oils. Typical marker crudes are West Texas Intermediate (WTI), Brent (North Sea), Arab Light and Edmonton Par Crude. As the price of marker crude moves up or down, other crude oils in the geographic area also move up and down, depending on their properties and on relative supply and demand.

Maximum efficient rate (MER): The maximum rate at which natural gas and crude oil can be produced without excessive decline of reservoir energy or a loss in ultimate production.

Measurement-while-drilling (MWD) tool: Technology that transmits information from downhole measuring devices to the surface while drilling is ongoing.

Medium crude oil: Liquid petroleum with a density between that of light and heavy crude oil.

Methane (CH$_4$): The simplest hydrocarbon and the main component of natural gas; methane is also produced when organic matter decomposes.

Midstream: The processing, storage and transportation sector of the petroleum industry.

Migration: The movement of natural gas, crude oil and/or water through porous and permeable rock.

Mineral rights: The rights to explore for and produce the resources below the surface. In the petroleum industry, mineral rights can also be referred to as "land."

Miscible flooding: An oil-recovery process in which a fluid, capable of mixing completely with the oil it contacts, is injected into an oil reservoir to increase recovery.

Mousehole: A hole drilled to the side of the wellbore to hold the next joint of drill pipe to be used; when this joint is pulled out and screwed onto the drill string, another joint of pipe is readied and slipped into the mousehole to await its turn.

Mud: Colloidal suspensions of clays in water or oil with chemical additives that is circulated through the well bore during rotary drilling.

Mud motor: A downhole drilling motor that is powered by the force of the drilling mud pushed through the motor by the mud pumps at the surface.

Multiple entry: A technique for drilling several horizontal wells from a single vertical, directional or horizontal wellbore.

Multiple zone well completion: Completion of a well in such a way that production is obtained from several different formations.

N

Naphtha: A light fraction of crude oil used to make gasoline.

National Energy Board (NEB): The federal regulatory agency in Canada that authorizes oil, natural gas, and electricity exports; certifies interprovincial and international pipelines, and designated interprovincial and international power lines; and sets tolls and tariffs for oil and gas pipelines under federal jurisdiction.

Natural gas liquids (NGLs): Liquids obtained during natural gas production and processing; they include ethane, propane, butane and condensate.

Nitrous oxide (N$_2$O): A very potent greenhouse gas which has a large number of natural sources and is a secondary product of the burning of organic material and fossil fuels.

Non-associated gas: A reservoir where only natural gas is found.

Non-conventional crude oil: Crude oil that is too thick to flow in its natural state and cannot be produced by traditional means.

O

Octane: A performance rating of gasoline; the higher the octane number, the greater the anti-knock quality of the gasoline.

Oil sands: Naturally-occurring mixtures of bitumen, water, sand and clay.

Operator: The company or individual responsible for managing an exploration, development or production operation.

Organic theory: The most widely accepted theory explaining the origins of petroleum: as organic materials become deeply buried over time, heat and pressure transform them into hydrocarbons.

P

Packer: An expanding plug used in a well to seal off certain sections of the tubing or casing when cementing and acidizing or when a producing formation is to be isolated.

Paleontologist: A person trained in paleontology – the study of plant and animal life in past geological time through the study of fossil plants and animals, their relationship to present-day plants and animals and their environments.

Palynologist: A paleontologist who specializes in fossil pollens and spores.

Pay zone: The producing part of a formation.

Perforate: Make holes through the casing opposite the producing formation to allow the oil or gas to flow into the well.

Perforating gun: A special tool used downhole for shooting holes in the well's casing into the producing formation.

Permeability: The capacity of a reservoir rock to transmit fluids; how easily fluids can pass through rock.

Petrochemicals: Chemicals derived from petroleum that are used as feedstocks for the manufacture of a variety of plastics and other products such as synthetic rubber.

Petroleum: A general term for all the naturally occurring hydrocarbons – natural gas, natural gas liquids, crude oil and bitumen. (This is the definition used by the National Energy Board and many other authorities. However, some industry and provincial authorities use a narrower definition of petroleum as meaning only crude oil; for example, some provinces issue "petroleum *and* natural gas" licences.)

Pig: A cylindrical device inserted into a pipeline to inspect the pipe or to sweep the line clean of water, rust or other foreign matter; pipeline inspection and cleaning devices are called pigs because early models squealed as they moved through the pipe. A "smart pig" is also equipped to find corrosion, cracks or weakness in the welding.

Pinnacle reef: A conical formation, higher than it is wide, usually composed of limestone, in which hydrocarbons might be trapped.

Pipeline: All parts of the physical facility through which gas is moved in transportation, including pipe, valves, and other equipment attached to the pipe, compressor units, metering stations, regulator stations, delivery stations, holders, and fabricated assemblies.

Pool: A natural underground reservoir containing an accumulation of petroleum.

Pooling Agreement: When the boundaries of two or more oil or gas leases do not coincide with the drill spacing unit, then a pooling agreement is needed among the lease holders before the regulatory authority will grant a drill permit.

Porosity: The volume of spaces within rock that might contain oil and gas; the open or void space within rock – usually expressed as a percentage of the total rock volume. Thus porosity measures the capacity of the rock to hold natural gas, crude oil or water.

Potential resources: The volume of natural gas or crude oil that is thought to exist based on geological knowledge, but has not been proven to exist though geophysical techniques or drilling.

Precambrian: Formed prior to the Cambrian era approximately 600 million years ago.

Primary recovery: The production of oil and gas from reservoirs using the natural energy available in the reservoirs and pumping techniques.

Probable reserves: Hydrocarbon deposits believed to exist with reasonable certainty on the basis of geological information.

Production casing: The last string of casing set in a well; production casing is tubular steel pipe connected by threads and couplings that lines the total length of the wellbore to ensure safe control of production, prevent water from entering the wellbore and keep rock formations from "sloughing" into the wellbore.

Production tubing: Steel pipe inside the casing used to flow the petroleum from the producing zone to the surface.

Productive capacity: The estimated maximum volume which can be produced from known reserves based on reservoir characteristics, economic considerations, regulatory limitations and the feasibility of infill drilling or additional production facilities; also known as available supply.

Prospect: A geographical area that exploration has shown contains sedimentary rocks and structures favorable for the presence of crude oil or natural gas.

Proved reserves: Hydrocarbons in known reservoirs that can be recovered with a great degree of certainty under existing technological and economic conditions; the category of natural gas reserves that have the highest probability of being produced. Generally, the reserves have been "proved" to exist with drilling evidence. In Canada some authorities use the term "established" reserves.

Public consultation: The process of involving all affected parties in the design, planning and operation of a seismic program, an oil or gas well, pipeline, processing plant or other facility.

Public interest: Usually intended to mean the interest of the public generally as opposed to the interest of an individual or company.

Q

Quad: An energy quantity of one quadrillion BTUs (1,055 petajoules), which is approximately the energy equivalent contained in one trillion cubic feet of natural gas.

R

Rathole: A slanted hole drilled near the wellbore to hold the kelly joint when not in use; the kelly is unscrewed from the drill string and lowered into the rathole.

Raw natural gas: A mixture containing methane plus all or some of the following: ethane, propane, butane, pentanes, condensates, nitrogen, carbon dioxide, hydrogen sulphide, helium, hydrogen, water vapour and minor impurities. Raw natural gas is the gas found naturally in the ground prior to processing.

Receipt point: The location where gas enters a transporter's system from a well, plant or pipeline interconnect.

Recoverable resources: Hydrocarbon reserves that can be produced with current technology including those not economical to produce at present.

Repressuring: Forcing gas, under pressure, into a crude oil reservoir in an attempt to increase the recovery of crude oil. This can also be achieved using water.

Reserve life index (RLI): The reserve life index measures the length of time current proved or established reserves would last if current production rates were maintained and no new reserves were added. Essentially, it measures the "ready inventory" of crude oil or natural gas. Also known as reserves-to-production (R/P) ratio.

Reserves: The recoverable portion of resources available for use based on current knowledge, technology and economics.

Reservoir (pool): A porous and permeable underground rock formation containing a natural accumulation of crude oil or natural gas that is confined by impermeable rock or water barriers, and is separate from other reservoirs.

Residuum: A heavy, black, tar-like substance that remains after crude oil has been fully refined to distil all usable fractions or components.

Right-of-way: A strip of land, the use of which is acquired for the construction and operation of a pipeline or some other facility, may be owned outright or an easement taken for a specific purpose.

Rod string: A string of steel rods used to provide up-and-down motion for a bottom-hole pump to lift oil to the surface.

Rotary bit: The cutting tool attached to the lower end of the drill pipe of a rotary drilling rig. The bit does the actually drilling of the hole through the formation.

Rotary drilling: A method for drilling wells using a cutting bit attached to a revolving drill pipe.

Rotary rig: A modern drilling unit capable of drilling a well with a bit attached to a rotating column of steel pipe.

Rotary table: A heavy, circular casting mounted on a steel platform just above the rig floor which rotates the drill string and thus turns the bit.

Royalty: The owner's share of production or revenues retained by government or freehold mineral rights holders. The royalty is usually based on a percentage of the total production and the rate may vary according to the selling price.

S

Salt cavern: An underground natural gas storage cavern which has been developed in a salt dome by the solution mining process.

Sandstone: A compacted sedimentary rock composed mainly of quartz or feldspar; a common rock in which oil, natural gas and/or water accumulate.

Secondary recovery: The extraction of additional crude oil, natural gas and related substances from reservoirs through pressure maintenance techniques such as waterflooding and gas injection.

Sedimentary rocks: Rocks formed by the accumulation of sediment or organic materials and therefore likely to contain hydrocarbons.

Seismic surveys: Refers to studies done to gather and record patterns of induced shock wave reflections from underground layers of rock: used to create detailed models of the underlying geological structure.

Set casing: To install steel pipe or casing in a well bore. An accompanying operation is the cementing of the casing in place by surrounding it with a wall of cement extending for all or part of the depth of the well.

Service rig: A truck-mounted rig, usually smaller than a drilling rig, that is brought in to complete a well or to perform maintenance, replace equipment or improve production.

Shale: Rock formed from clay.

Shale shaker: A vibrating screen for sifting out rock cuttings from drilling mud.

Shrinkage: The reduction in volume of wet natural gas due to the extraction of some of its constituents, such as hydrocarbon products, hydrogen sulphide, carbon dioxide, nitrogen, helium and water vapour.

Shut-in well: A well that has been completed but is not producing. A well may be shut-in for tests, repairs, to await construction of gathering lines, or better economic conditions.

Smart pig: Sophisticated instrument packages sent through pipelines to test for corrosion and buckling.

Solution gas: Natural gas is dissolved into crude oil in the reservoir.

Sour gas: Raw natural gas with a relatively high concentration of sulphur compounds, such as hydrogen sulphide. All natural gas containing more than one per cent hydrogen sulphide is considered sour.

Sour oil: Crude oil containing free sulphur, hydrogen sulphide or other sulphur compounds. Sour crude oil generally contains more than 0.5 per cent sulphur.

Spudding in: Beginning to drill a well.

Steam-assisted gravity drainage (SAGD): A recovery technique for extraction of heavy oil or bitumen that involves drilling a pair of horizontal wells one above the other; one well is used for steam injection and the other for production.

Steam injection: A technique in which steam is injected into a reservoir to reduce the viscosity of the crude oil.

Stimulating the formation: A technique for improving production from a reservoir; stimulation may involve acidizing, fracturing or simply cleaning out sand.

Straddle extraction plant: A gas processing plant located on or near a gas transmission line that removes natural gas liquids from the gas and returns it to the line.

Sulphur: A yellow mineral extracted from petroleum and used for making fertilizers, pharmaceuticals and other products.

Sulphur dioxide (SO_2): A poisonous gas formed by burning hydrogen sulphide (or other sulphur compounds).

Surface casing: The first string of casing put into a well; it is cemented into place and serves to shut out shallow water formations and as a foundation for well control.

Surface rights: The rights to work on the surface of the land.

Sustainable development: Development that meets the needs of the present without compromising the ability of future generations to meet their own needs (as defined by United Nations World Commission on Environment and Development).

Sweet crude oil: Crude oil containing less than 0.5 per cent sulphur.

Sweeten: Remove hydrogen sulphide and carbon dioxide from sour gas to make it marketable.

Sweet gas: Raw natural gas with a relatively low concentration of sulphur compounds, such as hydrogen sulphide.

Synthetic crude oil: A mixture of hydrocarbons, similar to crude oil, derived by upgrading bitumen from oil sands.

T

Tertiary recovery: Crude oil recovery using intensive techniques, such as steam flooding or injection of chemicals, to increase recovery. *See primary recovery* and *secondary recovery.*

Tight sands gas: Natural gas that is found in geological formations with low permeability.

Top drives: Hydraulic or electric motors that are suspended in the derrick above the rig floor to rotate the drill string and bit.

Traps: A mass of porous, permeable rock – sealed on top and both sides by non-porous, impermeable rock – that halts the migration of oil and gas, causing them to accumulate.

Tripping: The process of removing the drill string from the hole to change the bit and running the drill string and new bit back into the hole.

Trunk lines: Large-diameter pipelines that transport crude oil, natural gas liquids and refined petroleum products to refineries and petrochemical plants; some trunk lines also transport refined products to consuming areas.

U

Unconventional gas: Natural gas that requires specialized technology to remove it from the ground. Unconventional gas sources are generally categorized as tight sands gas, shale gas or natural gas from coal. The distinction between unconventional and conventional gas is becoming less clear.

Underbalanced drilling: Using mud lightened by the addition of nitrogen or other gas to minimize damage to the producing reservoir by drilling fluids.

Unitization: Process whereby owners of adjoining properties pool reserves into a single unit operated by one of the owners; production is divided among the owners according to the unitization agreement.

Upgraded crude oil: A blend of hydrocarbons similar to light crude oil produced by processing bitumen or heavy oil at a facility called an upgrader. (Also called *synthetic crude oil*.)

Upstream: The exploration and production sector of the petroleum industry.

V

V-door: The opening in the derrick opposite the drawworks used for bringing in drill pipe and casing from the nearby pipe racks.

Vibroseis: The process of producing seismic shock waves with "thumpers" or vibrator vehicles.

Viscosity: The resistance to flow or "stickiness" of a fluid.

Volatile organic compounds (VOCs): Gases and vapours, such as benzene, released by petroleum refineries, petrochemical plants, plastics manufacturing and the distribution and use of gasoline; VOCs include carcinogens and chemicals that react with sunlight and nitrogen oxides to form ground-level ozone, a component of smog.

W

Wellbore: A hole drilled or bored into the earth, usually cased with metal pipe, for the production of gas or oil.

Wellhead: The equipment used to maintain surface control of a well.

Well-logging instruments: Instruments lowered into a well to provide specific information on the condition of the well.

Western Canada Sedimentary Basin: Canada's largest region of sedimentary rocks; the largest source of current oil and gas production.

Wet gas: Raw natural gas with a relatively high concentration of natural gas liquids (ethane, propane, butane, pentanes and condensates).

Wildcat: A well drilled in an area where no oil or gas production exists nearby.

Wireline logging tools: Special tools or equipment, such as logging tools, packers or measuring devices, designed to be lowered into the well on a wireline (small-diameter steel cable).

This glossary has been enriched by the inclusion of new terms, courtesy of the Canadian Energy Research Institute (CERI).

Index